The Shadow in Our Lives

One family's recovery

from child sexual abuse

TRACEY WILSON
HEISLER, MA

The Shadow in Our Lives
One family's recovery from child sexual abuse

Published by
Tracey Wilson Heisler
New Jersey

Cover design: Eric Labacz, labaczdesign.com

For my children and any of yours that have been touched by the scourge of child sexual abuse. May they heal and break generational curses.

Contents

Introduction and Acknowledgements

This was an extraordinarily emotional and difficult memoir to write. It has not been an easy task, putting our family's trauma on full display, but I believe if there is anything in our experience that could help another family recover, then I wanted to share it. My children agreed and gave me their permission to share our story.

The names of all individuals have been changed except for my ex-husband and the investigator who handled our case, Ralph Garrett, as their participation in these events is a matter of public record. My recollections may differ from those of the others who shared those experiences as our perceptions are our own realities.

Each chapter has a "What I learned" and "What I would have done differently" section. Appendix A is a "Helpful Tips" sheet; an "Additional Resources" guide is listed as Appendix B.

I want to thank my friends Barbara, William, and Nicole for their editing eyes and my friend Ranae for her unfailing encouragement in telling this story. Thank you, too, to my friend Sherri for forging the publishing path for me to follow.

I also want to thank my sweet husband for his love and support as I revisited dark places in the past. Dredging up those memories has not been easy, but he was always there when I came back to the present. I could not have written this without his support.

Most importantly, I want to thank my children for trusting me to tell our story with the hope of helping other families. I am grateful for their faith and confidence in me and pray it was not misplaced.

Hindsight is always 20/20, and if I had the gift of foresight none of this would have ever happened. Tragically, it did happen to my family and while we have largely recovered, even today we still sometimes find jagged shards of trauma. I hope that our experience can be of some use to others who are trying to figure out how to best help their children and their family through this horrific experience.

I dedicate this work to those who have suffered most and who have been so generous and selfless in their willingness to share that suffering in the hopes of helping others: Diana, Marek, Angus, Bella, and Jared.

Tracey Wilson Heisler, MA

CHAPTER 1
Day 1

Fact: Only a third of children who have been sexually abused disclose it. Most never tell.

It was October 31st, 2003—Halloween. The kids had just gotten home from school, and we were getting ready to go trick or treating. My husband, Dale, was traveling from a military base where he worked on their endangered species management team, to the local community college where he taught Biology and Anatomy/Physiology as an adjunct professor. As was his custom, he called me en route to talk about his day and to see how things were at home. On this particular day, he was full of complaints about our eldest child, "Diana."

Specifically, he was upset because he had been asking her to clean her room for a few days now, and she was ignoring him. While this would not necessarily be surprising for most 15-year-olds, it was unusual for Diana, who was generally an amiable and helpful person. After hearing his speech about respect for parents, needing to get jobs done, etc. etc., I assured him I would speak to her about it and hung up the phone.

I went and found my daughter, who was not her usual self.

"What's going on with you?" I asked. "I just got off the phone with your father, and he says that he's asked you repeatedly to clean your room and you've been disrespectful and rude to him. That's not like you. What's the problem?"

No answer.

"Whenever your grandparents or I ask you to do something, you get right on it. Why are you being like this with your dad?"

Still no answer.

I pressed her on the point, wanting to find out what the problem was and fix it. We had five children, ages six to 15, and a busy life. I had just graduated with my BA degree in Psychology and had entered a master's program in Counseling Psychology. I also worked full-time, and Dale worked full-time plus the part-time teaching job. We didn't have time for drama.

"What's going on, Diana?" I asked her. Up to this point, she had not made eye contact with me. Now she looked at me with eyes filled with tears and reached for a poem she had been writing. This was not my confident and self-assured child. I knew immediately that something was dreadfully wrong. Reading it, my heart froze in my chest.

> *"Forever Hurting"*
>
> *Leave me alone. Just go away. I don't like you anyway.*
>
> *Back up. Keep your filthy hands off me. Don't make me do this again, please.*
>
> *What would you do if I told? I would watch your life unfold,*
> *your life of lies shatter into dust.*
>
> *I know that I must do something to ease this pain, calm the fear.*
>
> *I can't seem to let anyone near. All I know now is fear, no thanks to you.*
>
> *Are you happy, happy with what you've done to me?*
>
> *You've hurt, corrupted, lied to, and killed a part of me every day.*
>
> *Are you happy with what you've done to me? You've ruined my life, destroyed my chance for happiness, tried to twist my perception of reality.*
>
> *But it hasn't worked. I'm too strong for you. Do you know that?*
>
> *You tried to hurt me, but I still won. Bruised and battered, hurt and crying inside.*
>
> *I came out the victor but maimed for the rest of my life.*
>
> *Do you know what selfishness buys? Each time you are near, a part of me dies,*
>
> *remembering your sins against God, against me,*

against your unknowing family.

*What would they do if I told them? Would they
believe me? Do you care?*

*You were living your own personal lie and no
matter how hard I try I don't think I will ever get you
to realize your sins.*

*Self-righteous and proud, hypocritical in any
crowd. You think the world of yourself.*

*You think what you did was good. You are killing
yourself, too.*

*You have killed everything noble and good
inside of you, if there ever was such a thing in you,*

Listen to me now because I tell you true.

I don't know what mom ever saw in you.

"Sometimes he touches me, and I can't take it anymore," she
blurted.

In that moment my world shattered. I immediately grabbed her
and hugged her as tightly as I could, stroking her hair and telling her
it was going to be okay.

Until the months prior to that moment, if anyone else had told
me that my husband had abused a child, particularly his own
daughter, I would not have believed them. I had been with this man
for nearly 17 years. He was my friend, my love, and someone I had
until recently trusted implicitly. Because it was Diana telling me
this, I knew it was true. My worst fears as a parent had come true.

I continued to hug her and reassure her that I would handle this.
My first instinct was to maintain control of the situation by carrying
on as normal for everyone's sake. It was Halloween, and the other
kids were getting ready to go trick-or-treating. I didn't want to take
that from them, and I wanted to keep Diana from free falling. If I'm
honest, I needed to keep myself from free falling too. I told her not
to worry but to go get ready. We would take the kids trick-or-
treating, watch a scary, old, black and white B movie, and eat
popcorn and candy like we always did on Halloween. Since Dale
was teaching that night, he would not be home until close to 10 p.m..
By then everyone would be in bed, and I would deal with him.

So that's exactly what we did, in that order. Everyone got ready to go trick or treating, the younger kids excited about going and oblivious to what was going on. Diana was understandably distracted. She looked so worried, so scared because her secret was now out in the open. I hugged her again at bedtime and reassured her that her father was not coming into the house, that night or ever again. She would be safe. Reluctantly, she got ready for bed and headed for her room.

TEN MONTHS PRIOR TO THIS, Diana had casually informed me that she had seen her father looking into the bathroom window from the outside. She had asked me to talk to Dale about it so the neighbors wouldn't think he was a weirdo, which I did. His response was so reactive that it clearly hit a nerve—he had actually been peeping. It drove us to therapy for several months, which had only recently ended. Throughout that process he had sworn that he had never acted on anything—he struggled with inappropriate thoughts but had not acted on them. Finding out that he had was a gut punch. I had struggled to believe his denials in therapy and had come to accept his assertion that he hadn't crossed that line. Clearly, I was wrong, and so was the therapist.

I waited for the headlights to pull into the driveway and met Dale as he was getting out of the car. "You can't come in," I told him as he stepped out, his hands full of his teaching materials and his lunch bag.

"What do you mean I can't come in?" he asked, looking bewildered.

"Diana told me what you did," I told him, "and you aren't coming back in the house until this is all sorted out. I will notify the authorities in the morning, and you are going to have to go talk to the police and explain what happened. You have to make this right."

"I thought we dealt with this in therapy," he responded with some irritation.

"That was when I thought it was just a thought, not an action. You crossed a line, and you lied about it," I responded with disgust and contempt.

"But I didn't do it," he responded.

"You have to work this out with the police," I reiterated. "You have to tell the truth about what happened, for Diana's sake. But you aren't coming in here tonight."

"Well, where am I supposed to go?" he asked.

"You'll have to stay at a hotel. I will call you in the morning after I make the police report, and you will have to go to the station and talk to them."

He got back into the car, a look of fear moving across his face. Dale hadn't had so much as a parking ticket in his 41 years, and he had a dread fear of getting into trouble, of people with criminal histories, and of jails. He was terrified.

As he drove off, I went back into the house. I locked all the locks, and I put chairs under the doorknobs. I didn't have any fear of him harming any of us, but I did think he might try to come in and "reason" with me in the night since I told him I planned to call the police in the morning. He didn't.

What I learned

- It was vitally important for my daughter that I believed her immediately. I have since learned that less than four percent of child sexual abuse allegations are false, and rarely do those false allegations come directly from the child—it is other adults who make them. I read in one study that the average age of disclosure of child sexual abuse is 42. Most victims rarely tell anyone else about what happened to them. If they do, according to another study I read, it's usually because someone outside of the family took them out of the home and asked them directly about the abuse.

- It was equally important that I create a sense of safety and security for her. She was terrified of the repercussions of disclosing.

- While my own heart was broken, I needed to keep it together for my children's sake. Melting down, crying, screaming, etc. would have traumatized them and made my daughter feel like she had done something wrong in telling me what happened.

- Diana needed me to put her first, and I did.

What I would have done differently

- In retrospect, it was risky for me to have confronted Dale by myself. It could have ended badly. I should have called the child abuse hotline or the police that night instead of waiting. It would have provided a record of what happened (just in case) and it would have afforded law enforcement and not me with the opportunity to handle him when he got home.

- I had been reassured in counseling that while these had been thoughts in his head, he had not expressed them through physical actions. The therapist and I were wrong to have believed him and should have explored the possibility that he had acted on these impulses more thoroughly. Neither of us had wanted to alert Diana to this ugly possibility, and she had not disclosed anything to that point. In the end, the therapist and I took him at his word, which was a mistake.

CHAPTER 2
How Did We Get Here?

*Fact: Family members are responsible for approximately 30%
of all child sexual assaults*

In December 1986, I was 20 years old and living in my home state of New Jersey, readying myself to leave for school at a religious college. I had converted at age 14 and was an active participant in my faith until my family moved to Florida at age 16, where I didn't fit into my new congregation. I didn't go to church for the two years I was there. During that time, I was making some pretty poor choices and decided to move back to New Jersey in 1985 for a new beginning. Part of that new beginning was to start over and go back to church.

"Joanne" had been my best friend since middle school, and she and her parents very generously allowed me to stay with their family while I got on my feet. In addition to Joanne, they had three sons. With their help, within a few months I had a studio apartment, a job as a billing clerk in a doctor's office, and I was back in good standing at church. I also acquired a new boyfriend, Joanne's older brother, "Stephen." Overall, life was pretty good.

For more than a year I focused on work, Steven, and applying for scholarships to go to college. I had known Steven for many years, and over time I was falling more deeply in love with him. We had mutual interests in sci-fi and music, listening to ELO and The Cars for hours while driving around in his little red Triumph Spitfire. We took trips to Amish Country and hiked around in the Delaware Water Gap. We watched *Dr. Who* on PBS and *Conan the Barbarian* and *Clan of the Cave Bear* together. We just enjoyed being together. I felt like he could be "The One."

However, one of the major tenets of my faith was to marry another member in good standing. Steven would come with me to church and church activities, but it wasn't for him. He would not and could not embrace the testimony that I had, so I knew in my heart that I would not and could not marry him. As I struggled to figure out what to do, I became fixated on two things: I had to go to college, and I had to marry someone of my faith.

I applied for and received an academic scholarship to the school of my choice and was scheduled to begin classes in January 1987. When I told Steven about my decision—to move and go to school—he was supportive and accepting of it. He helped me buy new suitcases, refinished the floor of my apartment because my high heels had put dings in the wood, and drove me to the airport when it was time to leave.

I knew I wasn't coming back, but he didn't. I had decided a few months before to not say anything about breaking up because I thought it would be kinder to let the relationship die a natural death with me gone. I carried the guilt of how I handled that ending for many years afterwards. Not only had I hurt him, but I also damaged my relationships with his parents and his sister, whom I loved too. I took the coward's way out instead of being honest.

I had arranged for an apartment, sight unseen, before I left so that I had a place to go. A New Jersey friend, Samuel, planned to pick me up from the airport, but a weather inversion delayed my flight for 24 hours. Not willing to wait that long, another girl and I hitchhiked a ride from two businessmen to my final destination. From my current perspective as a parent, this was both stupid and dangerous. Fortunately, these two kind gentlemen delivered us without incident to our destination.

This was in the days before cell phones, and I called Samuel from a pay phone in Wyoming to tell him when I would be arriving. He was horrified at the risk that I had taken and was relieved to find me safe when the car pulled up and I was in one piece. We stayed at his grandmother's house that night, and the next day he took me to my new apartment. Everyone was gone for the winter break; he was leaving too, to go to his parents' home in Massachusetts. He made sure I had what I needed and promised that he would be back in two weeks. I was now alone over the Christmas holidays in another state where I knew no one.

There were few people in town as most of the students had gone home for the holidays. I went to the movies (*Little Shop of Horrors*), checked out the local businesses in the hopes of finding a job before the other students returned, and looked in the paper to see what activities were going on. I'm a social person by nature and sitting alone in an empty apartment waiting for my five new roommates to come back was not appealing to me.

One of the staples of life in my faith is the "fireside"—a gathering of believers where someone gives an inspirational talk. It is usually followed by food and fellowship. I attended one on Sunday night with a Christmas theme, introducing myself to the others in attendance. Everyone I met that night was welcoming and kind, but I can't for the life of me remember any of their names except for one: Dale. He was 24, good looking: short, very fit, highly intelligent, and oddly dressed. Think 1970s disco, not 1986.

Dale was a different sort. He could talk for hours about any number of topics, but his real passion was animals. I learned that he had a BS in Zoology and was working on his MS in Zoology too. He wanted to get a PhD in Wildlife Ecology and work with endangered species. He played the piano, he sang, he was a ballroom dancer, and a marathon runner—a man of many interests and talents. He looked so young, though, more like 17 than 24. He had to show me his driver's license to prove his age because I didn't believe him.

As the fireside ended, I invited the others in the group over to my apartment to play board games, which we did. Dale chose not to kill me in Risk and let me win. It was about midnight when everyone but he left; we stood in the doorway and talked for two more hours. It was a snowy December, and the apartment was freezing because I had the door open for two hours. We clicked.

Throughout that whole week we spent nearly every waking hour together, sometimes with the others from the fireside and sometimes just the two of us. We looked at Christmas decorations and lights, "duck walked" down the street with exaggerated strides, and went snowmobiling. He invited me to his parents' home for Christmas, an invitation which I gladly accepted. He came from a large family—nine brothers and sisters—and they made sure that there were gifts for me under the tree. Dale calculated that the number of hours we had spent together that week was the equivalent of dating once a week for six months. We both were thinking the same thing—we had found our other half. As is encouraged in our mutual faith community when making an important decision, we fasted and prayed about whether to get married. Both of us felt inspired that this was the right thing to do. So, one week after we met, Dale and I got engaged.

As we discussed our plans for the future, he became serious and said he needed to tell me something. His father, David, had "acted inappropriately" with one of Dale's sisters, Dawn. As an adult, she disclosed what had happened as part of an ecclesiastical interview, which triggered police and church involvement, but because it had happened years before the case was closed with no charge or consequences. David had been the leader of the congregation in his local church, not once but twice, and because no criminal charges were filed there were no significant church sanctions either.

Their family had briefly gone to counseling to address the situation at the time. There were no details given, and it was a closed matter as far as they were concerned. He just thought I should know about it before we got married. I accepted the disclosure and didn't share it with anyone else; it wasn't my secret to tell, and it didn't affect me or my new little family. He had been open about it, and I didn't have any concerns about it happening to us.

We called my parents to tell them of our engagement, and they were aghast. My mother yelled (a lot), to the point that Dale wouldn't let her speak to me because I was so upset by it. This infuriated her. She called Steven in New Jersey to tell him what I had done, which broke his heart. I was then filled with anxiety about that. I hadn't meant to hurt him, and he didn't know that I had moved on in my head and in my heart months before. My new roommates, who had returned from the holiday break and heard the story of what had transpired, held an intervention to try to dissuade me from marrying Dale. I didn't know any of these five women before moving there, and their concerns held no weight with me. Apart from his family, no one else seemed happy that we were engaged.

However, I was determined that this was the person I was going to marry, and I did marry him two months later, in February of 1987. My parents declined to come, and only a long-time family friend, Erica, my great-aunt Frieda, and Samuel attended in support of me. Dale had dozens of friends and family members who came, so it was a festive celebration in the end.

Despite the upset, I was incredibly happy and felt like my life was going in the right direction. I was active in my faith, I was married to another church member whom I adored and who adored me, and I was ready to have children. In fact, I was desperate to have children and raise them to be righteous, kind, and loving people who would be of service. I gave up my academic scholarship because now the focus needed to be on getting Dale through his MS program and into a PhD program. I was 20-years-old.

NOW CHANCES ARE GOOD that you are reading this thinking, "What in the hell is wrong with this girl? This is the stupidest thing I've ever heard." In retrospect, getting engaged after a week was exceptionally stupid, especially given how badly it all turned out in the end. However, I was young, inexperienced, and felt like I was doing what God had intended for me to do. While it was an anathema to my family and friends who did not share my faith, this is not unheard of in my church culture. Lots of young people in that space meet, fall in love, and marry within months. There is such an emphasis on sexual purity that engagements tend to be only a few months long. I recognize that this situation is an outlier even within the Bell Curve of an evangelical culture. That said, I really did feel inspired that this was the person I was supposed to marry. I believed that God had worked out all the challenges for my good.

From the time of our marriage in 1987 through the fast forward to 2003, we had five children in nine years, "Diana," "Marek," "Angus," "Bella," and "Jared." Dale finished his MS (1988) and PhD (1992) degrees and did postdoctoral research at the Museum of Natural History in Washington, D.C. (1992-1994). He then took a job as a contractor with a firm that focused on the ecological management of military lands. When his grant funding ended in October 1996, he became profoundly depressed. I went to work full-time while he stayed home taking care of the kids and researching and applying for jobs. After more than a year of looking, he took a position that he viewed as a step down at a military base in Florida as part of the endangered species management team (1998).

From the beginning of our marriage, my focus was on our family. I stayed at home and raised our children, helped Dale get through school, and contributed to our income where I could. For years I had an in-home daycare during the day and worked as a typist and editor for students and authors at night in the years preceding the widespread use of in-home computers. I also waitressed on evenings and weekends. I did what I could to contribute to our household income and eventually opened a preschool with a friend in 1999. I felt continually prompted to go back to school, so I enrolled in the local college and graduated with my BA in 2003.

Dale and I went to church every Sunday and volunteered our time as teachers and leaders there. We took family vacations every year. We worked, paid our bills, took the kids to the movies, and had regular date nights. We bickered some but rarely fought. Dale would create scavenger hunts for me on Valentine's Day and my birthday. I made sure Father's Day, his birthday, and Christmas were special for him. We cooked and cleaned, made homemade bread, and had a garden, canning salsa, whole tomatoes, and pickles. I volunteered at our children's schools, and he helped them with their science fair projects. We made plans. We bought a Prius. Friends came over regularly for dinner and game nights. It was a normal, busy life.

When Dale's grant ended in late 1996, the regular rhythms of our family life began to change. I went out Christmas shopping with a friend. I got home late, and everyone was already in bed. As I passed through the living room, I noticed that the red light on the VCR was on, indicating that something was being recorded. I was curious as to what it was and turned the television on. It was porn, a channel which I later learned was part of our cable subscription. I was devastated. I had found porn periodically over the years, and Dale knew it was something that hurt me deeply. More fundamentally, it was a sin in our evangelical world. I woke him up, yelled at him, cried, broke open the VHS tape, and pulled the guts out, destroying it.

I slept on the couch that night and went to speak with a friend the next day, seeking counsel about what I should do. She and her husband recommended getting counseling from our ecclesiastical leader, which we did. It would help for a while, but the pattern of using porn in times of stress, me finding it and freaking out, and then me trying to get Dale to go to counseling repeated every few years or so. We also canceled our cable subscription so he wouldn't be tempted by media with sexual content, opting instead for movie nights from Blockbuster. Our family didn't have television again until after Dale was arrested in 2003.

What I learned

- While I am someone who has always relied on inspiration from God for guidance, there is a good chance that I mixed in what I wanted here. Where does personal desire begin and revelation from God end?

- Never get engaged to someone after a week, no matter how much time you spend together during that week. You really do need time to really get to know someone, their family, and their culture. (Duh!)

- I had just come back into full fellowship in the church and didn't feel particularly worthy. I was very young with an idealized version of what my life should be. My primary support system of family and friends didn't understand how much I relied on what I believed God wanted me to do, so I didn't believe they could possibly understand my perspective. I should have realized that He had sent me objective and concerned individuals to help me with this big decision. I just didn't hear their voices.

What I would have done differently

- I should have been less entrenched in the narrative in my head about what my life "should" be based on my cultural expectations of marriage and babies first, school second.

- At the time, I believed that if I had stayed in New Jersey and married Steven, I would be settling for less than I wanted. I should have been more focused on my education and personal growth than on a romanticized view of life and relationships.

- I should have listened to those people who I knew loved me and were concerned for me.

- I should not have gotten married.

CHAPTER 3
The Months
Before the Disclosure

Fact: Most child sexual abuse occurs at home, 84% for children less than 12, and 71% for children 12-18

At the time of Diana's disclosure in 2003, Dale and I had been married almost 17 years and, except for the periodic stress induced porn usage, had a close and happy relationship—until January 2003. Diana had just turned 15. One day, she came to me and said, "Mom, you need to talk to dad. He was looking in the bathroom window from outside, and the neighbors are going to think he's weird."

When Dale got home that night, I mentioned her comment to him and asked him what he had been doing. He had a look of panic on his face, said he didn't want to talk about it, and stormed out of the house. When upset, he was prone to tantrums like this, never violent or physical, but would make a scene and storm out. I didn't know then what the issue was, and I wasn't particularly concerned about it. He sometimes got offended at stupid things, particularly if he felt as if he were being criticized – this time was likely not any different.

This time was different, however. He was gone for two days. After he didn't come back the first night, I recognized the seriousness of what was happening and analyzed the situation more critically. Why was he looking in the window? It must have been for a bad reason, or he wouldn't have run like that. Had this happened before? Had he molested Diana? Was he contemplating it? Were the other children in danger? What was going on?

In a moment, the life I thought I knew was suddenly in jeopardy. I gently and subtly started asking my daughter questions. If nothing had happened I didn't want to shock or scare her. If something had happened, I needed to give her an opening to tell me about it. Had she seen him do anything like this before? It was weird, wasn't it? What possible reason could he have had for peering in the window? She was noncommittal: Who knows why he was doing it? He just needed to stop doing it.

When he finally returned, I asked him if he was ready to talk. He told me that he had come close to committing suicide, that he had been out in a field ready to do himself in. I was unimpressed with and dismissive of his dramatics. I could see this for what it was, an attempt to manipulate me into feeling sorry for him and giving him a pass on whatever was going on.

It wasn't until much later, after the relationship ended, that I recognized to what a great extent he had been emotionally manipulative throughout our relationship. For many years I had given what I now see were bad behaviors a pass, choosing instead to be more loving, more understanding, and more forgiving. I believe that this was the first time in our relationship when I refused to accept his deflections and kept pressing for answers.

I asked him again, "Why were you peering in the window?" No answer. "Were you trying to peep at Diana?" Fidgety movements and darting eyes. "Were you?" In retrospect, I don't think he ever acknowledged what he was really doing. His lack of an answer told me what I needed to know. He had been trying to peep at his own child.

"Have you ever touched her?" was my next question.

"No, of course not," was his emphatic answer.

With no hint of impropriety from my conversations with Diana, I wanted to believe him. I was overwhelmed with grief and fear, but absent any physical abuse, I thought the situation was salvageable. I did not know how long this had gone on and to what extent, but it had to stop now.

I was in the final semester of my bachelor's program, and as a student at the university I had access to the counseling center. Therapy was a must. With five children, student loans, and a house to run, we had never been well off, and the cost of therapy had been a barrier in the past. While I had found mental health resources for Dale's depression off and on over the years, he never went for more than a handful of sessions, citing the cost and ineffectiveness of the treatment. This time was different. I gave him an ultimatum: Go to therapy or we're done. In addition, if I found any indication that he had inappropriately touched Diana or anyone else in any way, we were also done. He accepted my terms.

I was taking evening classes that semester and working part-time during the day. However, I no longer felt safe leaving the children with their father while I was gone. I didn't tell anyone else what was going on; I didn't know if my marriage and our family could be saved or not, but I certainly wasn't going to advertise that my husband had been peeping at his own daughter and we had to go to therapy because of it. As a result, my support system during that time was limited. I skipped a lot of classes while struggling to keep up with the work. It was my last semester and I needed to get it done. I called on friends to see if the kids could come over for a few hours or asked my parents to come over and hang out because "Dale had lots of work to do and can't really supervise that well." By that time, he was teaching in the evenings and often had papers and tests to grade.

We went to therapy from January through August 2003. The therapist, a woman, saw us separately and together. I don't know what she and Dale talked about, but it was clear in the months to come that he had not been open with her about the reality of his actions. He minimized them or did not disclose them. In my sessions the focus was less on me and more on strategies to deal with Dale's depression, open communication, creating a safe space where he felt he could talk to me, and rebuilding trust in the relationship.

I remember one memorable session when she posed the following question: "How can you still have an intimate relationship (which had been suspended for some months but had recently resumed) with someone you know has sexual thoughts about his own daughter?"

It was a good question, and one that I had struggled with myself. My answer was that so long as he had not crossed that line—from a thought to an action—there was still hope of salvaging our relationship and keeping my family intact. She was satisfied with that answer, but it is something that has always haunted me. I loved this man, built a life with him, created five beautiful children with him, and considered him my best friend before all of this. How could any measure of trust and intimacy ever be rebuilt?

The therapist tried her best to help, and I thought that we were successfully completing therapy. I was to learn that her efforts had been ineffective because Dale had not been open with either her or me. From my perspective she, like me, had been unwilling to press him on the uglier possibilities and instead took him at his word regarding the extent of the abuse. Like me, she thought the relationship was salvageable. I have since learned that there are clinicians who work exclusively with sex offenders and are adept at calling them out when they are being emotionally manipulative or minimize their actions. We needed one of those.

With these new revelations, my primary question became, "How could any of the good remain knowing how tainted the foundation of this marriage is?" In sum, it couldn't. My hopes for a happy ending with repair and restoration were shattered in just a few short moments on that fateful Halloween night.

What I learned

- Therapy is an essential part of getting help for both the offender and the victim.
- Therapy only works in rebuilding relationships if all the participants are engaged, want help, and are transparent.
- While open communication, trust, and a safe environment are crucial to healthy relationships, when one of the partners is manipulative or has a secret agenda, they will use this openness, trust, and safety against you.
- It is likely that a person who has committed an act of child sexual abuse will not be completely truthful about what happened. They often minimize or do not disclose their actions to protect their own fragile sense of self-esteem and avoid criminal prosecution.

What I would have done differently

- I wish that I had recognized the importance of the red flags that were evident prior to Diana's offhand comment about Dale looking in windows. In retrospect, there were some areas of concern that I now wish I had followed up on.
- I should have pressed Diana harder about whether anything had happened to her. While I tried to give her an opening to tell me what had happened, I didn't want to be transparent about this abhorrent possibility with her. In the end, she carried this burden for far too long because she was worried about the impacts to the rest of us. I should have been more open with her about what I was really asking and created a safe space for her to talk, if not to me than to someone else.
- Given the information I had at the time, therapy was the right thing to do. However, I should have found a therapist who was more suited to this type of family trauma. Ours was a marriage and family therapist, which sounded right at first, but the depression, the sexual dysfunction, and the inability of either her or me to detect that Dale was lying called for greater expertise. Not every therapist is the right fit for the situation. It can take time to find the right person to help.

CHAPTER 4
Days 2 and 3

Fact: Only 55% of child sexual abuse reports are investigated. The rest are "screened out."

After a sleepless night of crying and praying, I went about figuring out what to do next. I oversaw our family's finances, so I changed the pin numbers on our credit and debit cards, limiting Dale's access to our joint funds. I was worried he would drain the accounts. He still had keys, and I knew that Diana was worried that he would come back. While she had been nonchalant about the peeping, now that everything was out in the open, she was terrified. She wanted him caught and locked up immediately. She wanted to feel safe. I went to the hardware store and bought new locks first thing.

My parents lived nearby, and while I had told them that we had had a fight, I had not yet disclosed what the underlying reason for it was. My mother was a survivor of child sexual abuse, and she was a strong and forceful person who often overreacted to even minor events. I needed to remain in control of the situation, and I didn't want to tell them what was happening until I was ready to tell them.

My father and I swapped out the locks while my mother pestered me for details of what was going on. I remember her joking with my father that no matter how many fights they had been in over the years, she'd never felt it necessary to change the locks on him. It was unfathomable to them that I was taking such extreme steps, especially since Dale and I had always been so close. They were supportive, but it was clear that it was killing my mom to not know what was going on. She made no secret of the fact that she had never, ever liked Dale.

A few years before, when Diana was about 12, my mother had raised the possibility of something going on because Dale sometimes napped in Diana's room at our previous residence, saying that it was quieter than our room. I pooh poohed it as her being paranoid but did pop in unexpectedly a handful of times, just in case. Nothing going on but Dale sleeping and Diana doing homework, playing with her hamsters, or reading a book. I dismissed it out of hand. One red flag. The peeping made two.

I called Dale's parents, alerting them to what was happening. They were terribly upset, but not for the reasons you may think. I knew before marrying Dale that his father, David, had molested his daughter, Dawn. After Diana's disclosure about Dale, I later learned that Dawn had not been the only victim. David had in fact molested all his daughters, each believing that only she and Dawn had been abused. They only learned the truth about their joint victimization when they started talking about what had happened in our family.

While each girl suffered, the way each coped differed dramatically. One turned to art, another to long hours at work, another to a life of service, one was drawn to fringe ideologies, and the last one became hyper-religious. From the outside looking in, they are successful, happy, and productive adults today. They work hard, they are active and involved at church, they serve their community, and they love and care for their families. They view their father as a good man who had a flaw. He taught them how to be productive, hardworking, good people, and the fact that he wounded them is less important to them than his other contributions to their lives. They have forgiven him, they love him, and they miss him (he has since passed away).

From my vantage point, while David may have given much, he took much more. The scars of the abuse still exist, even if the anger, the hurt, the betrayal, and the broken trust are hidden away. I liken it to a filthy closet that is kept closed so the neighbors can't see in.

The damage done to Dawn was irreparable. In a discussion with David after Dale's actions became known, he told me that he felt what he had done was analogous to him cutting her off at the knees emotionally; and it was. She married late in life and died an early, painful death from cancer only a few years later, leaving an eight-year-old son. I still mourn for her and what her life could have been had this not happened to her. The burden of carrying on as if nothing had happened, the overriding Christian mandate to forgive, to move on, to keep peace in the family, etc. took its toll on her, body, and spirit. Her sisters still struggle too, no matter the composed face they outwardly share.

Over the years I have thought about how their family handled Dawn's disclosure. With no police action or public embarrassment, their mother, Cordelia, decided to stay. I don't think to do otherwise ever really crossed her mind. Her method of dealing with the reality that her husband had molested her daughter was two-fold: 1) blame her daughter for her part in "enticing" him and 2) follow him around everywhere to ensure that he didn't do anything to his grandchildren, most of whom did not know of their beloved grandfather's past bad actions. It was never talked about openly within the family, although I have since had candid individual conversations with most of Dale's siblings and with both of his parents about the impact the abuse had on their family.

I never left my children alone with David and Cordelia; Dale or I were always present. Nothing was ever said about it, but I knew that David understood my position. He was many things, but chief among his gifts was the ability to read people. He knew that I knew, and he never once challenged me on it. My parents were extremely upset with me when it became known that I never told them about David's past abuse. At the time, I didn't feel it was my family secret to share with anyone, and I was keeping my children safe. In retrospect, perhaps I should have been more open about it. He didn't directly hurt my children, but his abuse of his children indirectly did.

Because I had cut off Dale's money, my thought was that his next course of action would be to go to his parents' home. Surprisingly, he had not yet contacted them. I rang them first thing Saturday morning.

I learned some disturbing things during that phone call. His mother's first reaction—no lie or exaggeration here—was to say, "Well, at least he didn't get her pregnant!"

I was horrified. While I had known about David's abuse of his daughters, I still had a cordial relationship with him—he was a very engaging and genial man who was unfailingly polite to me and helpful to our family. Cordelia was blunt and sometimes abrasive, but I always worked hard to treat her with kindness and respect. Over time I came to see that David, this charming, affable, and likable man, oftentimes set Cordelia up to look like the bad guy.

Because her emotional intelligence was low and her interpersonal skills were limited, she often seemed mean, cold, and difficult. There were days when she was hard to like, and the day of that call was one of those days.

Both David and Cordelia disclosed during that call that they too had been victims of child sexual abuse as children, David at the hands of a boarder in his parents' home in the early 1940s. Cordelia had been abused by someone in her family. She never said more than that, not how old she was, what type of abuse, or by whom, just that she had been molested by someone in her family. This conversation taught me so much about intergenerational abuse, the devastating impacts of family secrets, and how deeply rooted the dysfunction was within this family. They understood exactly what had happened in my home. The difference was that no one in their culture or their family would ever consider reporting it or enforcing consequences for it.

I asked them not to aid Dale if he came looking for help. I needed him to turn himself in to the police and let the matter go through the system. They agreed, but I think they were amenable because they had not fully thought through the consequences to their son. Their future actions showed that while they knew what he had done was terribly wrong, their preference would soon be to "keep it in the family" to spare him the societal, economic, and familial consequences of his actions. In the months and years to come, they would pay for attorneys, house him, feed him, and pay his bills. He became their responsibility all over again until the day each of them died.

I had learned about the abuse Friday night. I spent Saturday changing locks, cutting off Dale's access to our money, and notifying his parents. I kept reassuring Diana that everything would be okay. My other children had not yet picked up on the fact that something was dreadfully wrong. It wasn't unusual for their father to be gone for long periods of time; he had a full and a part-time job as well as his volunteer work at church. Ironically, I worked in the child protection system and wanted to speak with a colleague and church friend, Drew, who handled these kinds of cases before I made the call but had not yet made contact with him.

That Sunday morning, I went to church and tried to talk to

Drew, who worked as a caseworker for the Department of Children and Families (DCF). I wanted some guidance from him on whether to call the police first or the DCF child abuse hotline. I worked with an organization that provides advocacy services for children who had been abused or neglected, and we often shared cases. As it happened, Drew thought I wanted to talk about work and put me off, leaving me to make the decision on what to do without input. Sunday afternoon I called in a report to the Department of Children and Families' child abuse hotline instead of the police. Drew later apologized for deferring the conversation. He had not realized this was personal, not professional, for me.

It wasn't long before an investigator, Ralph Garrett, came out, along with a Deputy Sheriff to take the report, interview Diana and me, and decide what to do. Investigator Garrett is a tall, deep voiced, confident, and intimidating figure. If he were to question you about something, you would absolutely pay attention. He spoke with authority, and I knew that once he got the chance to interview Dale, he would surely confess. With Diana, he was unfailingly kind, compassionate, and reassuring. She trusted him immediately. Investigator Garrett is one of the heroes in this story. Diana is the other.

Dale had yet to resurface, but I knew it would only be a matter of time with his limited resources. There was a child advocacy center near where we lived, so Investigator Garrett scheduled a time later in the week for Diana to have a formal forensic interview. Because I worked in the child welfare system, a DCF investigator from an outside office handled their part of the investigation. In the end, no action was taken against me as I was a non-offending parent, had made the report in a timely manner, and was cooperating fully.

Monday was fast approaching. I called my children's school principals (elementary, middle, and high school) to ensure that they knew that something was going on, although I didn't specify what, and to make sure that they would not release my children to their father should he come by to get them. I hadn't spoken with Dale since Friday night, but he is a very smart man. He had to know there would be consequences, and I thought he might try to take some of the children for leverage. The schools, to my dismay, refused to keep the kids from their father should he try to pick them up because there was no court order in place barring contact. I decided to keep all of them at home. I couldn't take the risk of him coming to get them.

Day three ended with all of us hunkered down at home with me finally telling my parents and the other children what was going on. I started with just my parents. I wanted them to know the full story and the truth of where we were. My mother kept exclaiming, "I knew it! I knew that little bastard was no good! I told you!" My father kept muttering, "I'll kill him. I'll beat the shit out of that little bastard. I'll kill him." I told the kids separately, saying only that "Dad hurt a child, and he can't come home right now." Bella and Jared cried. Marek and Angus looked worried and concerned. Diana was stoic. It was a terrible, truth-telling day.

What I learned:

- It was important for me to be methodical in my approach to dealing with this devastating disclosure.
  - Focus first on my family's safety;
  - Stay in control of the situation – while there were many well-meaning people who might want to jump in and assist, at the end of the day my children needed me to be their leader and protector. They needed me to be the anchor for them;
- I needed help to work through my feelings. I was devastated by the realization of the disclosure and the crisis that it presented. I didn't have time to emotionally process what was happening. That would come later.
  - I needed to maintain my boundaries and keep my children's safety – not my heart and my fear – at the forefront;
- Family secrets run deep. There were things I didn't know about that contributed to the situation, like the other sisters' abuse and Dale's parents having been child sexual abuse victims themselves.
- I have a greater respect for survivors' instincts when it comes to certain people or situations. They are usually spot on in their assessments, not paranoid in their thinking. My mom was right on the money about Dale and who he was. She saw him much more clearly than I, and she recognized him for who he really was. I wrongly dismissed her concerns.
- Families will circle the wagons to protect their loved ones, even when they know they are wrong. It's abhorrent, but it happens all the time. Dale's parents and many of his siblings would ultimately choose him.
- Cooperating fully with the authorities helped Diana and me as her parent. Investigator Garrett told me that I was only the second mother in 20 years of working child sex crimes to immediately believe the child, take steps to protect them, and cooperate fully with law enforcement from reporting through prosecution. By being transparent and supportive of the process, no action was taken against me, my kids didn't end up in foster care, and our family stayed intact.

What I would have done differently

- I would have called in an abuse report to DCF that first day. While I was committed to making the call from the first, I wanted time to think it through. I shouldn't have waited.

- My daughter, Bella, recently told me that she thought I should have been more open with her and her siblings earlier. She realized her father was gone, she saw what was happening with the locks, she heard my parents and me talking, and she saw Diana's apprehension and fear. All this caused a lot of anxiety for her. I should have told them sooner what was happening.

- Other than that, I believe my actions were correct. I was trying to accomplish these three objectives, and I did:
  o To keep Diana and the other children safe;
  o To make sure Diana knew that I believed her and would protect her;
  o To get Dale to turn himself in and face the consequences.

CHAPTER 5
Day Four

Fact: Child molesters look and act like everyone else and are at church, school, and youth sports.

Day Four since the disclosure passed much the same as Day Three. I kept the children home from school again, and we treated it like a Saturday. I took another day off from work, the kids watched movies, and I cleaned and cooked. I tried to stay busy while I waited for the other shoe to drop—for Dale to resurface. Until that happened, life couldn't just go on. I had circled my wagons to keep my family safe and would continue to do so until he was in custody.

My parents got to the house by 6:30 in the morning. I think they were concerned about our safety, although they didn't articulate that. Throughout the day my mother processed the news as I knew she would. She needed to talk about it. "I knew it!" she exclaimed repeatedly throughout the day. "I never trusted that no-good little bastard right from the beginning. And at dinner I would look him in the eye and say to myself, 'I'll kill anybody that ever touches one of my grandchildren,' and he just sat there looking at me like he was an innocent. That little bastard better hope I never see him because I will kill him!"

Alternatively, my generally passive father kept muttering, "I'll beat the shit out of that son-of-a-bitch if I ever see him." Like me, they were devastated. Like me, they were there trying to protect the children, who were bewildered by the sudden vitriol against their father, as much as they could. As soon as the local furniture store opened they went out and bought me a new bed, mattress, and box spring. My mother insisted that the old one had to go, and I was glad to get it out of the house and onto the curb in time for garbage day.

The person who hurt my heart the most was eight-year-old Bella. She adored her father, and she was starting to miss him. She kept asking me, "Where's Daddy? I miss him. When can I see him?"

My father and I sat down with her to explain again that Daddy had hurt someone and couldn't come home. She didn't believe us, so I told her that he had hurt a child. She refused to believe us and walked around carrying Dale's picture and crying for her father. I have rarely seen my father cry, but he and I both cried many tears that day. Our hearts were broken for her, and we cursed Dale anew for this fresh hell. How do you explain something so vile to an eight-year-old?

It was clear that my initial attempt to give Bella as little information as possible because the truth was just so ugly would not be acceptable. I was a little more forthcoming this time. Daddy hadn't hurt just any child, he hurt Diana, and he wasn't a safe person to stay in our family. Because the child he had hurt was her sister, who confirmed that it was true, her mournful cries for her father diminished. She loved her father, but she loved her sister, too. Between Diana's affirmation and her grandfather's and my reasoning as to why Dale couldn't come home, she accepted the situation. That's not to say that she didn't stop missing him or that she loved him less, she just understood that it wasn't possible. We didn't tell her more expansively what he had done until later, in a therapeutic setting. I just wasn't sure I had the words to give her that she needed to hear.

My older son, Marek was playing on the computer that afternoon when his father messaged him, trying to find out what was happening and whether "it was safe to come home." Marek told me immediately—I honestly don't remember if I had him answer or if I told him to ignore it and not give him anything. A friend of mine remembers Dale messaging Diana and telling her that she had ruined the family with her disclosure, but I do not have a recollection of that. I did call Investigator Garrett with the Sheriff's Department to let him know that Dale was resurfacing and looking for information. He suggested that he install a recorder on the phone so that if Dale called, I could try to get a confession out of him. He showed me how to work it and provided me with a backup cassette just in case he called and I filled up the first tape.

As I said in the beginning, Dale and I had been exceptionally close. I thought that we were each other's best friends. We talked often throughout the day and debriefed at night about all kinds of things—the children, church, work, the news—everything. He was my biggest fan who told me that I was beautiful, smart, and that he was so lucky to be with me. Here I was, plotting with the Sheriff's Department to record our next conversation to gather evidence against him for what I knew he had done, sexually abusing our precious daughter.

During these early days it was like the world had flipped upside down into an alternate universe, like the "Upside Down" in *Stranger Things*. Every day I tried to be strong for my children, to be the leader they needed me to be and to keep them safe. Every night I lay in my bed sobbing. I cried for my lost husband, for the love I thought we had. I cried for my daughter and the abuse she had suffered. I prayed for a way to keep both the husband and the daughter that I loved in my life. I struggled with the many hurts and injustices of this new reality.

I am ashamed in retrospect of how much I mourned the loss of him. He wasn't worth my tears, but I definitely had to have a transition time to move from wife-in-a-loving-and-happy-marriage to angry-and-bitter-ex-wife-who-wanted-to-castrate-and-kill-him. Maybe it was the loss of my dreams that I mourned most, the perfect life I had envisioned for myself. Bottom line: I loved him deeply and I deeply hated what he had done. It took me some time to accept that he wasn't the man I thought he was, and we didn't have the relationship I thought we had. It had been a sham. It took me a long time, too long, to accept the truth. I hate his betrayal of everything I thought we had built. I was a sucker.

As I anticipated, he called home that night. I was ready. We talked for more than two hours, so long that I had to pop in the new cassette tape into the recording device Investigator Garrett had left me to make sure I got everything. I tried to do it as quietly as possible so he would not suspect what I was doing. He went from denial to acknowledging some inappropriate touching, to justification, to an acknowledgement of inappropriate actions, absent any details. I did not want to know any of what happened, I still don't, but suffice it to say that I got enough from him that it wouldn't take much effort from a prosecutor to convict him.

He wanted to come home; I told him again that he couldn't. He needed to turn himself in to the police and explain what happened, for Diana's sake and for all our sakes. We couldn't go back to the life we had until this was addressed. It was, of course, a fairy tale to think that any of this could be fixed, but I needed him to think he could regain what he had lost if he turned himself in. He agreed to think about it, although it was clear that he was very afraid of the consequences – not for us, but for him. He had never been in any trouble, and the thought of any kind of involvement with law enforcement frightened him.

What he and I both knew was that he was running out of options. The kind and loving wife that he had had for nearly 17 years wasn't nearly as helpful as he had anticipated. He had little money, and his parents weren't giving him anything to help him escape. The net was closing, and he knew that facing the charges was his only real choice. I think he still had hope that, like his father before him, he would walk away with a slap on the wrist, his family and reputation intact. My emphasis on "make this right" made him think that things could go back to the way they had been. In reality, there was never the possibility of a restoration of our former lives. My only goals at that point were to make sure my children were safe, for the abuse to end, and to see justice served by making him accountable for his actions. For that to happen, he needed the hope that he could walk away from this. He needed to trust me, one more time, to help me accomplish those goals.

What I learned

- I never realized how manipulative Dale was throughout our marriage until it ended. I always thought of him as someone with limited social skills who was inexperienced and unsophisticated, highly intelligent and driven when something interested him. I didn't recognize how calculating he could be. It took me some time to see that it was I who was the naïve one, and that my weakness was the flattery and affirmation that he provided. Now I look at everyone as someone who could be a predator.
- I learned to separate my love for someone from the realization that they can do bad things.
- By sharing information with law enforcement in real time, they were able to help me with tools to gather evidence to help my daughter. Had there been things like photographs, text messages, video, etc. it would have been much easier to convict. The best I could do was an audiotaped confession, but it was a needed contribution.
- Being honest with your loved ones, especially your children, is not easy but it is necessary. By trying to protect their delicate sensibilities, you leave open the potential for the predator to manipulate them too. Knowledge is power – I learned that I had to share it in doses that are appropriate to the child's age and cognitive abilities.
- I had to forgive myself for loving and trusting my husband and mourning his loss after learning about his crimes. I am both deeply ashamed of myself and understanding of my thought processes simultaneously. I acknowledged what I lost, but I also have come to understand that we are all so much better off in the end without him. I didn't see who he really was until it was too late.
- God does not want us to be in abusive relationships, whether it is us or our children who are being hurt. He wants us to be safe, to be happy, and to be loved.
- No matter how hard, my daughter and my other children had to be first. Period. End of story.

What I would have done differently

- I would have let my kids see me struggle more. A therapist told me some years later that by keeping all my sorrow and struggles to myself, I unknowingly sent my children the message that they couldn't openly process what they were feeling, that they needed to "man up." I thought I was being strong for them, but in reality I was too strong, they needed more honesty from me about how this impacted me and my life. It could have served as a model for them on how to process life's trials in a healthy way.

CHAPTER 6
Day 5

Fact: Arrests are made in only 29% of child sexual abuse cases; for children < 6, it is only 19%.

It was now Wednesday. I had kept the kids out of school on Monday and Tuesday and decided to do it again. Dale was still out there, and if our conversation from the previous evening was any indication, he was getting desperate. He had no money and no allies that I knew about. Aside from our family, he was a loner with few friends. He knew that my non-negotiable demand for him was for him to turn himself in, and so I waited.

My parents had not yet come over, but I knew they would be soon. It was mid-morning, and I was cleaning up. Bella and my youngest, Jared, had been playing outside for about a half an hour when they burst into the house. "Daddy's here!" Bella chirped with delight. I was frozen for a moment. "What?" I said. "Your dad's here?"

"Yes, he's right outside!" she said excitedly. "He told me to come get you because he wants to talk to you."

Diana had heard her sister's announcement and ran into her room, hiding under her bed. She was so scared, her face white and her eyes large. "Don't worry," I reassured her. "He's not coming into the house. Lock the doors behind me. It's going to be okay, sweetie. I promise."

Dale had parked his car around the back of the house. He looked terrible, unwashed, haggard, and scared.

"You can't be here," I said. "You need to go."

"I don't have anywhere else to go," he replied.

"Well, you can't stay here. My parents will be here soon, and if my father sees you, he's going to beat the shit out of you. Seriously."

"I don't know what to do," he said.

"I told you what has to happen. You have to turn yourself in.

This isn't fair to anyone, but especially not to Diana. She is scared out of her mind. You have to make this right."

There was silence for a moment. He wasn't convinced, so I went on. "How about if we drive to town? I'll rent you a hotel room for a couple of days, you can get a shower while I get you some lunch, and we'll go to the sheriff's department together. How does that sound?"

"Okay," he replied. "But you'll stay with me, right?"

"I'll go with you, but I think we should take two cars. I'll have to get back to the kids after you get settled."

Little did he know that I too was terrified. There was absolutely no way I was getting in a car with him; he was too unstable. I had underestimated him, thinking that his response to this situation would be one of reason and cooperation. I was wrong. But I also recognized that this was the opportunity that I had prayed for, to get him into police custody so the kids and I would be safe.

"Give me a minute to get my purse. I'll be right back," I said. I went back to the side door and knocked, calling out that it was me. Marek opened the door to let me in and quickly relocked it behind me. I called for Diana to come out.

"I've convinced your father to go with me to town so he can turn himself in at the sheriff's department," I told her as she entered the room. "I need you to watch the kids while I'm gone. I'll call Oma and Opa (my parents) and let them know so they can get over here."

My beautiful, smart, and remarkably brave daughter was pale and drawn. This was taking such a terrible toll on everyone, but most especially her. She strongly identified with the character "Eowyn" in Lord of the Rings, and I think that this example had informed her disclosure. She was trying desperately to be brave. I wanted to protect her. I needed to keep her safe. I needed to get her justice. I needed to make her whole again. I grabbed my purse and my phone and hugged her goodbye. "I love you," I told her. "It's going to be okay. I promise."

I hurried outside, fearful that he had changed his mind and taken off again. But he was there, looking angry/scared/apprehensive—all of it. I got into my car and motioned for him to take the lead. I wanted to be able to see him in case he changed his mind.

Once I started driving, I anxiously fumbled for the phone. I was scared but determined to get him to the sheriff's department. I needed to call my mother to let her know the situation and ask her to get to my house as quickly as possible to be with the kids. While Bella had been happy to see her father, and Jared was too young to really understand what was happening, the other three were extremely nervous. They understood the gravity of what was happening. They needed the reassurance and protection of trusted adults. As I drove away from the house, I berated myself for my stupidity for letting the younger ones play outside. What if he had taken them? I pushed the thought aside to focus.

After a few rings, my mom answered the phone. I quickly filled her in on what was happening. "You can't go with him!" she exclaimed. "Are you crazy? He could hurt you. You turn around and get home right now. Just call the police and have them pick him up!"

"I can't do that," I explained. "If I veer off, he'll know something's up and run. If I have the police pick him up, he'll just clam up. I need for him to think he's safe, that I'm an ally, for him to cooperate. Don't worry. I won't do anything stupid. Just get to my house, please."

Hanging up with her, I focused on the drive, which took about half an hour. Traffic was light, and there were no delays. I parked my car next to his once we reached the hotel. Getting out, I told him to wait in the car while I got a room for him. I reserved a room for two days. Once I paid and got the key, I escorted him to the room. He had an overnight bag with him.

"You look awful," I said. "You go get cleaned up and get dressed. I'll run out to Subway and get you something to eat before we go to the Sheriff's office."

"You're coming back, right?" he asked suspiciously.

"Of course I am," I said. "What kind of sandwich do you want?"

With his lunch order in hand, I headed out to Subway. While it may have seemed that I was just getting lunch, I was desperate to get out of the hotel room. Not only was I scared of what he might do, I was disgusted to be in the same room with him. I needed him to believe that all would be well if only he would talk to the police, explain his side of things, and then we could all go back to our lives. I needed him to trust me, but it was incredibly hard. I felt like I was going to vomit. I wanted to punch him in the throat, to scream at and spit on him, and to cry and to rage about the devastation that he had brought to all of us in his family. I wanted to kill him.

Instead, I gave him a reassuring smile and spoke in a soothing voice. I got him settled in his hotel room and headed to the restaurant where I ordered the sub, chips, and a drink. I drove back to the hotel and called Investigator Garrett from the parking lot to let him know we were on our way in so he would be there and be ready. I had already given him the tapes from the night before, so he had what he needed for the interview with Dale.

Lunch in hand, I got back to the hotel, using the second key to get in the door. Dale had just gotten out of the shower. He got dressed and ate while I waited, making small talk. I tried to mask my anxiety and rising fear. This was an ordinary exchange in an extraordinary situation. The sense that something had to break was palpable. Once he finished eating, I said, "Let's go." And, to my surprise, he did. My strategy of being calm, reassuring, and firm about what had to happen next was successful.

We again drove separately. The sheriff's department was quite close to the hotel, so the drive didn't take long. I know that Dale was scared too, scared of what the consequences were going to be. Once we got there we walked in together. I spoke for the both of us. "We're here to see Ralph Garrett," I said to the receptionist. "He'll know what it is in reference to." We sat down and waited, a seemingly united front.

"Do you want me to go in with you?" I asked Dale.

"No," he said. "I think I should go in by myself."

"Okay," I replied. "I'll be right here if you change your mind." We sat in silence until he was called. What else was there to say?

Investigator Garrett came out and looked hard at Dale. "Come with me, please." he intoned. With a nod to me, they disappeared into an interview room.

Alone in the waiting room at the sheriff's department, I started to shake. Since he showed up that morning, I had been so scared that he would do something violent. I had never anticipated that he would run, and I had never considered that he might hurt us until he fled. That action, coupled with Diana's disclosure, made me realize that I hadn't really known him at all and that I couldn't accurately predict what he would do. This man who shared my home, my children, my bed, and my dreams was a stranger to me. To finally see reality after having been so blind for so many years was sickening and horrifying. How could I have been that stupid for so long?

In that space between his reappearance and turning himself in, I worried that he would run again, that he would hurt me, that he would hurt the kids, or that he would hurt himself in front of us. The fear of violence at my husband's hand was foreign to me until that moment. The relief I felt to have delivered him to Investigator Garrett wasn't only emotional, it was physical. I started to cry, which I am sure startled those around me. I quickly headed to the restroom, trying to compose myself. The magnitude of what was occurring was suddenly sinking in for me. I was transitioning from crisis mode to reality mode. Maybe now we could move past this freeze frame we were living in.

Once I composed myself, I returned to the lobby and passed the time leafing through magazines, unable to concentrate on any of the words. I could hear the occasional wail emanating from the closed door. "He must be talking," I thought. "I wonder if Ralph got him to confess?"

After more than an hour, Investigator Garrett and Dale emerged from the interview room. Dale looked like he had been crying and was still wiping away tears from his red and swollen face. Investigator Garrett and I locked eyes. He crossed his wrists, and I nodded my head, understanding what was next. He planned to arrest and handcuff Dale, and I was fine with that. Dale saw my nod, and he too instantly understood. I had set him up, and now he was going to jail. The flow of tears stopped immediately, and he furiously yelled at me, "You set me up!"

"Yes, I did." I replied.

"Did you even plan to put me up in the hotel?!" he screamed.

"I paid for two days," I responded. And with that, Investigator Garrett took him away to be processed, Dale yelling at me and protesting his arrest. I believe he thought that he would be allowed to go home, pay a fine, do community service, go to counseling, and have his record expunged. His arrest seemed to come as a complete shock and surprise to him.

I went back to the hotel to collect his things and canceled day two of the reservation, then drove back to the Sheriff's Department and checked out his car, which was still in the parking lot. It was filled with camping gear, empty food wrappers, drink containers, winter clothing, maps of North Carolina and Tennessee, and bottles of urine. These possessions made it clear that Dale had planned to hide out in the mountains, à la Eric Rudolph. I would have to make arrangements with my dad for him to come back to town with me later to pick up the car and drive it back to my house. It's amazing how the everyday details of life, picking up and cleaning out a car, still manage to intrude on the drama that had just unfolded. Even amid a crisis, the mundane has its place.

I called home to check on everyone. My mother answered and I filled her in on what had happened. She was, as we all were, incredibly relieved that he was in police custody. I headed home and picked up my dad so we could drive right back to town and pick up Dale's car. I didn't want to risk a ticket by leaving it overnight at the sheriff's department. The stasis we had been living in was over, and the clock of our lives started ticking again.

What I learned

- Law enforcement was my ally in this. Cooperating fully and trusting the investigating officer was essential.
- My children's safety was of paramount importance. It was stupid of me to let Bella and Jared play in the yard with Dale at liberty.
- Having a support system, my parents in my case, was an important part of keeping my kids safe and helping me to assess the risks and benefits of my actions during a time of great volatility and chaos. Making important decisions in times like that can be risky.
- By cutting off Dale's resources, I forced him into a corner. This could have gone one of two ways: he would trust me to help him, or he would hurt me to get out. Fortunately for me, he chose the former. That said, he could just as easily have chosen the latter.

What I would have done differently

- I would have "hardened" our home. Specifically, I should have had my dad come to stay with us, which he offered to do, had the police keep an eye on the house, kept the doors locked, kept the kids inside, etc. What if Dale had absconded with Bella and Jared? What if he had come into the house? I doubted that he would come back, and so I didn't take the safety precautions I should have taken.
- I don't know if there is anything I could have done differently and not spooked Dale into running again, but I did make myself vulnerable and put myself at risk. I'm grateful that I stayed safe, but I can't say that that was guaranteed. It would have made my kids' lives even harder had I been hurt or killed.

CHAPTER 7
Next Steps

*Fact: Nearly 70% of **all** reported sexual assaults occur to children.*

Now that Dale was secure and the threat of harm had passed, I started thinking about next steps. I worked with Investigator Garrett on what the Sheriff's Department and the prosecutor needed to successfully take this to trial, which included an interview with Diana at the Child Advocacy Center (CAC). I had participated in these kinds of interviews before in my work as a child advocate, and the way this advocacy center handled them was brilliant. They created an atmosphere of safety and comfort for child victims.

When a child experiences a trauma, great care must be taken. If you ask questions about what happened you can inadvertently "lead" them to a narrative that may not be accurate, thus tainting the opportunities for the case to be prosecuted. If you ask the child to repeat what happened to different parties multiple times, you re-traumatize them with each re-telling. Evidence needs to be collected, but the process can be so difficult that many victims don't want to continue cooperating. This Child Advocacy Center had developed a best practice protocol that worked to minimize these negative outcomes.

The child and a forensically trained interviewer sit together in a child-friendly room. It is not sterile or intimidating in any way. There is a two-way mirror in the room with an unseen room adjacent where law enforcement, therapists, the Guardian ad Litem, the prosecutor—anybody who is on the child's team—can watch the interview and ask for further clarity from the forensic interviewer through an earpiece. The child never knows that all these people are watching and listening to them tell their story, asking questions, formulating prosecution or therapy strategies, and figuring out ways to help. And the child only has to tell the story once.

This team approach extended beyond the forensic interview with the sheriff's investigator, the therapist, the child welfare investigator, the guardian ad litem—all the child's team members—meeting together regularly to assess the child's needs, to identify gaps in services, and to share information as one unit. This approach, while more time consuming, enables each of these helping professionals to leave their individual silos and work together for the good of the child.

I had two appointments, one for Diana to be interviewed, and one for each of the kids to meet with a therapist. Once Diana was called in the other four kids and I waited in the lobby until it was our turn. The therapeutic support services that were offered at the CAC were short-term in nature. Because I had worked with them on other cases I knew what was available to us. My new goals included making sure that Diana was receiving therapy for the abuse, ensuring that none of the other kids had been victims, and making sure that everyone was getting needed support services.

Family members are never allowed to sit in on victims' interviews. Therefore, I was not a party to Diana's interview, nor did I want to be. Daily I live with the guilt of not seeing what was happening, and I know that knowing more would just eat at my soul. While Diana was in her interview a therapist from the Child Advocacy Center talked to each of my kids, one by one, to assess how they were doing. They were later individually interviewed by an investigator to determine whether Dale had ever done anything to any of them. None of the other four disclosed any abuse. I was grateful for that small mercy.

Investigator Garrett came out of the interview room to meet with me before Diana came out. "She did an amazing job," he told me. "That is one brave, smart, strong girl there. With her interview, we'll get a conviction. I have no doubt in my mind. She did as well in there as anyone I've ever seen."

I knew that was true. Diana was and remains a remarkable human being. As an aside, Investigator Garrett exemplified the absolute best of law enforcement. His focus on getting justice for my daughter, on preventing future acts of abuse, and his kindness and compassion toward Diana and me showed him to be a man of integrity and honor. We were so fortunate to have him on our case.

Once Diana came out of her interview, the therapist met with all six of us. We talked about how our family was going to deal with this moving forward. How would we explain to others who asked? Would we continue to cooperate with the police through prosecution? Would we engage in therapy individually or as a family? Was this going to be a family secret, or would we be open about it? Where would everyone's loyalty lie, with Diana or Dale? Was support for both possible?

Our family culture has always been a family council where everyone had a voice. This conversation was no different other than there was a therapist leading the discussion, and Dale had no say. This family council approach continued throughout the process, including when I was later asked by the prosecutor for input regarding sentencing and probation. We talked as a family with the kids having input as to what they thought was fair; our collective recommendations were shared accordingly.

We decided as a family that we were going to be open about what had happened. While we wouldn't advertise the abuse, nor would we lie about it or try to hide it. We didn't want any family secrets. Everyone agreed that our full love and support would be with Diana. While there were varying degrees of love and wistfulness for Dale, everyone agreed that Diana was and would remain the priority. We also agreed that family therapy, at least in the short-term, was needed. Diana agreed to go to individual counseling. I felt I could benefit from it as well. At the time I was in my master's program in counseling psychology, so I knew where and how to get help.

We attended our family counseling sessions at the Child Advocacy Center, and Diana attended individual sessions. Because it was short-term, we were expected to secure outside therapeutic services. A colleague of mine put me in touch with his wife, who was a counselor and volunteered to provide individual counseling for me and for Diana, free of charge. She said it would be her tithing. I gratefully accepted. Dale had been the primary breadwinner in our family and while I worked, I didn't have the resources to pay for therapy, which had seemed a luxury up until this point.

A month later I went to see my doctor for an illness, and she asked me about whether I had experienced any depressive symptoms. I told her that I was in the middle of a divorce and that I had periods of depression. She prescribed an antidepressant, which in the end I chose not to take. A few months after that my application for life insurance was declined based on a diagnosis of "depression" found in my medical file. I had to appeal this with the doctor, who removed it from my medical records, and I was able to get a life insurance policy to ensure that the kids would be okay financially if I were to pass away. This was an unintended consequence of being open about what was going on and what my needs were in recovery.

Money was another issue that had to be addressed. Up until this point I had no student loan debt; all the expenses for my BA and now my MA degrees were paid for by grants and scholarships. I had never accessed student loans, so now was the time. I was able to tap into $7,500 a semester, $22,500 for the year, to support my children. In addition, after I graduated with my BA, I had been offered a full-time case manager position for $29,000, for a total of $51,500 in annual income. While not the $63,000 that Dale brought in, it was enough to keep my kids in their home and my bills paid. In the immediate aftermath of Dale's arrest, his parents and some of his siblings donated a few hundred dollars a month when they could, which was a big help.

My parents were equally amazingly helpful and amazingly difficult during this time. They provided childcare and transportation, made dinner, helped with house cleaning and maintenance, and offered love and support to all of us. On the other hand, my mother sometimes had a hard time with boundaries. I came home to find my living room and kitchen had been painted. Another day I came home to find she'd bought a cat, which I never wanted to have (I still have one of her kittens), because my son Angus wanted one. She renamed our dog, from Gimli to Jack, because she thought Gimli was a stupid name (she is not a *Lord of the Rings* fan). In her effort to help, she was taking over. I think she saw my blindness where Dale was concerned as confirmation of my inability to make the right decisions for my family. While I know intellectually that she was trying to help, emotionally it was challenging. Her well-intentioned actions created unnecessary stress.

I recognize that in large measure my parents felt that they knew what to do better than I did. They could see that I was overwhelmed, and they felt like they needed to take charge in the same way that I felt I needed to take charge for my children's sake. It was a difficult time for everyone, and there was so much chaos that roles and responsibilities were not well defined. We all knew that we wanted to keep the kids safe, to get them the help they needed, to keep the bills paid, and to keep Dale in jail. How it got done was sometimes a mess with hurt feelings and angry flare ups. But, at the end of the day, we pulled together for the kids' sake.

The primary issues that had presented themselves since Diana's disclosure, safety, therapy, and money, were being addressed. It was an imperfect patchwork of solutions that were filling our immediate needs. What I didn't know then was how far-reaching and long-term these challenges were going to be. What we had in place would do for now, but longer-term solutions were going to be needed. Problem solving how to get out of this new crisis mode took a lot of time, creativity, and cooperation.

What I learned

- Utilizing the support systems in place to help is crucial. There is no need to go it alone.

- It was a good idea to make the solutions collaborative. There was so much emotional investment in what happened next for everyone that it was important for each one of us to feel like we had a voice in the solutions and next steps.

- Having a broad network of support is especially important. I needed to know who my allies were. You'll notice that mine were my parents, not anyone from church or my friends, most of whom lived far away. "Outsiders" just didn't know what to do, so they did nothing, nor did I ask them for anything. Being clear about how people can help and asking for help when needed will ease the burden of getting through each day.

- Leadership in a crisis is important. It would have been much easier if my parents had done what I asked without undermining me. That said, they may not have done so much if they hadn't felt like they were in charge of the situation. It was a tricky place to be. Determine what the leadership structure is going to be, and make sure the kids know who they can go to for help.

- Getting therapeutic help for everyone as quickly as possible is vital. A traumatic experience like this extends beyond just the abuse. The whole interpersonal family dynamics were changed, and the potential for things like victim blaming, idealizing the absent offender, and recriminations existed. We all needed therapy, not just Diana.

- Researching available resources – family, friends, church, social services, non-profits, etc. – and having a plan is essential, particularly if the offender is the primary breadwinner. Bills still need to be paid, people still need to eat - not having those needs met makes it tempting to recant and not cooperate with prosecution.

What I would have done differently

- I would have set clear boundaries with my parents in terms of roles and responsibilities. The lack of clear leadership added more stress than there needed to be and made things confusing for the kids. Who was in charge? That said, had I done that I ran the risk of them withdrawing or limiting their help. Open communication among the players is key, and we didn't have that.

CHAPTER 8
Justice

*Fact: 70% of child sex offenders have between 1 and 9
victims, while 20% have 10-40 victims.*

With Dale incarcerated, I let the children go back to school. His arrest and charge were in the newspaper, although the victim was not named. It didn't take a great leap to guess what had happened. The kids and I again met with the therapist from the Child Advocacy Center to discuss what our response would be when questions arose. To the community's credit, there were few who directly asked for details. We were both well-known in the community. I had owned a preschool in town a few years before, and there were a few panicked calls from parents whose children had attended as well as people from church whose children had taken piano lessons from Dale. People knew us and they knew what he had done, but they tended to keep questions and comments to themselves rather than subject the children or me to scrutiny.

One exception to this came several weeks later. A woman from church came to me to say that she had heard a rumor going around that I had caught Dale having sex with Diana. She expressed concern that this story was making the rounds and thought that I should know. I was enraged. Not only was that false, but the fact that there was some disgusting little gossip who was making up lies and then spreading them around, especially when we were all deeply wounded and struggling to stop the bleeding, sent me into a fury.

I thanked the person who told me about it and asked her from whom she had heard it. I then called that person, going backwards through the chain until I hit the source, a woman from church who I had known for years but was not someone with whom I was friendly, specifically because I knew she was something of a gossip.

By the time my inquiries got to her, my voice was shaking as I asked her if she had been the one who was spreading this information around. She started to answer, but before she could finish, I screamed at her, "Quit spreading lies about our family! This situation already sucks enough for my children without your nasty, made up stories! If you really want to know what happened, all you had to do was ask. We've been open about this, there is no need for you to re-traumatize everyone with lies. Shut your DAMN month, and if I EVER hear that you're gossiping about this with ANYONE there will be consequences. DO YOU UNDERSTAND ME!"

She squeaked out a "Yes," and I slammed the phone down. From that day on, no gossip made its way to me again. That's not to say it didn't happen, only that I never heard of it again.

One of the unexpected outcomes of having this be so public was the outpouring of well-meaning support that Diana received from so many women in our lives. With every, "I'm so sorry, it happened to me too," she began to perceive the world as a very unsafe, predatory place. It was the "Me Too" movement before the "Me Too" movement. Because so many of these ladies were people we knew from church she started to look differently at men in the church. I tried to get her to understand that child sexual abuse is a scourge that occurs in every community across the country. With estimates ranging from one in four to seven girls and one in six to 25 boys having been victims of child sexual assault, she was now part of a not-very-exclusive club. There is some research that suggests that one in four women and one in six men will be sexually assaulted over their lifetime. Sexual assault is a public health emergency that we cannot ignore and that we must address proactively.

My younger children, who had not reported the negative experiences that she had, were supportive of their sister but were also worried about their father. In my line of work, I had seen what happens when one parent cuts their children off from the other parent, whether the reasons are valid or not. The other parent often becomes a mythical, often longed-for figure. I didn't want Dale to become a martyr or "forbidden fruit," so I took any of the kids who wanted to see him to the jail where he was being held so they could see that he was okay. They were reassured to see him. He was deeply grateful for the visits, although he misinterpreted them. He thought it signaled that his family supported him and would be there when he got out. He was wrong. It was so they could move forward without him.

My parents and my siblings did not understand my rationale for these visits. I remember one heated exchange with one of my brothers, who was at my house with our parents. He started screaming at me that I had allowed this to happen to my daughter, that I had protected Dale, and that I was personally responsible for all that Diana had been through. He thoroughly disapproved of me taking the kids who wanted to go to the jail to see their father and expressed his opinion that I didn't care about my children's well-being and bore the responsibility for the current situation (note: it was not as polite a conversation as the synopsis implies).

I screamed back, using all manner of expletives at my disposal (which was not characteristic of me and thus more impactful), and threatened him with the police if he didn't get out of my house. He was not the first and certainly not the last to blame me for not seeing what was going on and holding me responsible for Dale's crimes. I took a lot of flak for the decision to let the other kids have contact with their father, but in the end I think it was the right one.

I also allowed him to write to them, although I read the letters first to make sure they were appropriate, and for them to write to him, for the same reason. Keep in mind that until that Halloween day, the other kids thought we had a safe, loving, and mostly happy family. They had not been privy to the peeping issue or to the fact that we had been in therapy for months. For the kids to lose their father was hard, and they weren't ready to sever that connection yet. And I wasn't yet prepared to be the person who made that decision.

Dale wrote to me, too, pretty much every day. He tried to remind me of the love he had for me and for our family, how he knew he had messed up, but it wasn't really his fault. He resurrected the long-term plans and dreams that we had and was trying desperately to get me back on his team. Many of the letters were crazy in ways that are difficult to describe—vivid dreams and fantasies, deep and dark depression, theoretical threats of harm to him by other inmates. They were exhausting. I confess, the toll these daily letters were taking on me emotionally and psychologically was debilitating. I felt an obligation to read them, but they were sucking my energy and keeping me tethered to the past.

Despite what had happened, I still loved this man. He was the father of my children. We had been together for 17 years and had built a home and a life together. Before the peeping, he was my best friend, and he and our children were my world. He had celebrated my successes and mourned my failures with me. He told me that I was beautiful, that I was smart, and that I was deeply loved. I had believed in him and what we had together. I had fought to save the relationship for the better part of the previous year and was finding it difficult to fully disconnect from him, even knowing what I knew. That took some time to do.

With time, introspection, and therapy, I have come to realize that I coped with the stress of daily life by developing a romanticized view of our life together. While there had been many good times and happy memories, there had been bad times too, as in any marriage. Dale could be short-tempered, ungrateful, and lazy. He was often selfish and self-centered. He was easily overwhelmed, to the point that I took on nearly all the responsibilities for keeping our family going – house, bills, appointments, school projects, and car repairs. Once he left our home, life went on as it always had because he had only been responsible for providing us with an income. He worked, as did I, but he was at his leisure at home. In retrospect, I was in many ways less his partner and more his mother. I was an enabler, and I was compensated by the compliments and the personal validation that I received.

I do not mean to imply that I was a paragon of long-suffering virtue. I too had my deficits that no doubt contributed to our marital troubles. I can be controlling, and I have a "fix it" mentality that probably undermined his confidence as a leader. If he didn't get it done, I did. I realized later that I was in a codependent relationship, which, according to Wikipedia's definition, is "a dysfunctional helping relationship where one person supports or enables another person's addiction, poor mental health, immaturity, irresponsibility, or under-achievement." That was it exactly. I made a lot of excuses and covered for his behaviors, and I felt like a martyred hero doing it. I got something out of the unhealthy part of the relationship.

I both anticipated and dreaded the letters. To get them meant that he loved and missed me. To read them meant that any healing or joy I had was being sucked away. One was particularly dark, with Dale threatening to kill himself because without his family, there was nothing to live for. It was deeply upsetting to me, and my parents could see it. This is one of the circumstances when my mother intervened without my knowledge or consent, and this time I was grateful. She called the warden at the prison where Dale was being held and told him that he was writing every day to the victim's home, and it was upsetting her. In the Florida justice system, it may not have been due process, but it was effective. The letters ended immediately. The kids knew they could write to him if they wanted to, but he wasn't to write to them or me. It was a profound relief.

With Diana's recorded forensic interview from the Child Advocacy Center, my audiotaped phone conversation, and Dale's interview with Investigator Garrett, the Prosecutor had more than enough to take the case to trial. Since Dale had so little experience with the criminal justice system, he was really at a loss. His parents got him an attorney who wisely advised him to take a plea deal, which he did.

He was arrested in November 2003, and he was sentenced by January 2004 to 46 months in prison. I spoke with the prosecutor about my concerns for his mental health and for our long-term safety. I was so pleased that she incorporated many of our collective concerns into the plea agreement, including mental health counseling concurrent with his probation post-release. The probation terminated once our youngest child, Jared, turned 18, so he would be supervised and have to participate in counseling for a term of 10 years after his release. While these provisions made him bitter, they offered me a sense of relief and safety.

Diana wanted to go to the sentencing hearing, but she didn't want Dale to see her. She was frightened of him but also wanted to see justice done. I was deeply grateful for the plea deal that negated the necessity of her testifying in open court. My mother wanted to go too, and since I worked at the courthouse, one of the bailiffs I knew was sympathetic to our desire for anonymity and secreted us in a balcony above the courtroom. We didn't sit in the seats where Dale could see us; we huddled on the floor with our backs to the wall, listening to the exchange between Dale and the judge.

The charges were read, as was Diana's poem, and the judge said that he understood from the prosecutor that a plea deal had been reached. Dale said "Yes, but" and started to go into an explanation for his actions, that he wasn't really guilty of this, there were extenuating circumstances, etc. The judge cut him off and asked if he wanted to go to trial. No, he would take the plea deal. His attorney must have explained that he risked far longer than 46 months in prison if a jury decided his fate.

Since his arrest in November, he had been held in the county jail, which was less than a mile from our house. We all passed it every single day—to school, to work, to the store, to my parents' house. Our reactions to these daily drive-bys were mixed. Some of us waved, some of us taunted, some of us ignored the absent husband and father who could not see us or our reactions. On the days that I was alone, I screamed, cursed, and threw up my middle finger when I passed by. I had so much anger, so much hurt, and so much rage that I could not express openly. These explosive outbursts, overeating, and violent action movies were my therapeutic releases.

I realized later that I had developed another coping mechanism as well: music. In the early days of our marriage, when I was so happy and ignorant, my life's soundtrack was "True Love Ways" by Buddy Holly. During Dale's deep depression, it transitioned to "Barely Breathing" by Duncan Sheik.

In the weeks after Dale's arrest, it was the song "I'm Moving On" by Rascal Flatts. The whole thing just seemed to me to encapsulate what I thought Dale must be feeling. The song is about a man whose mistakes have alienated him from his community, and he's made the decision to leave and move forward. The lines of this song resonated with me too. I believed that Dale loved us as much as his damaged heart could, but in the end it wasn't enough. We all lost so much because of his sins.

As time went on and I became more raw with anger, the songs were "Love Stinks" and "Kill Me, I Want to Die" as sung by Adam Sandler in "The Wedding Singer" and "The First Cut is the Deepest" by Sheryl Crow. As my rage grew, I was challenged to retain any sense of internal peace for myself and trust for others.

A year later, I had to do a practicum and internship for my master's degree. As it turned out, I ended up at the county jail for a year's rotation in the mental health unit working with adult offenders. Dale had since moved on to the prison system. During the interview process, I was open about him having been there in the prior year. The therapist remembered him well. He had been dubbed "The Crier."

Because of confidentiality and the professional ethics that go along with therapy, we never discussed anything about Dale's time in the unit other than that detail. But, knowing him as I did, I could only imagine what his time there had been like. He was a high-status professional who had never had any type of interactions with law enforcement, and now he was an inmate accused of one of the most heinous crimes known to man. In addition, he had never known privation, fear, or the kind of brutality and callousness that are inherent in incarcerated populations.

He had threatened to kill himself when he was first discovered peeping, so I would guess that he would have spent some time in isolation on the mental health unit. If that were so, he would have had his clothes taken from him and given a paper gown so he could not harm himself. The isolation unit, created for inmates at risk of self-harm, was also incommodious. In addition to the indignity of paper clothes, the tiny room has a bare cot with no blankets so you can't hang yourself. One wall is a glass window so you can be seen 24/7, and the room is kept very cold so it is too uncomfortable for malingerers to stay as a respite from the noise and crowds of the general population. The mental health unit is inhospitable at best.

Throughout his incarceration, Dale was moved to at least three different prisons. He was sent to one in the county, another one on the coast, and a third in the northwest corner of Florida. He had been evacuated from the one on the coast because of a hurricane; the flooding was too intense to keep the inmates there. I don't remember where I heard it, but he apparently tried to convince people that he was there because of domestic violence. Given that he's only 5'4" and was scared of the other inmates much of the time, his cover story wasn't convincing. Apparently, some of the inmates asked friends/family on the outside to look him up on the internet and found he was there for child sexual abuse. That bit of information prompted at least one of the moves.

What I learned

- People are going to gossip about what happened. You can't change it, but you need to find a way to cope with it.
- Justice in cases like this is rare. Diana was fortunate enough to have received a conviction and see a penalty in the crimes against her, but many victims do not. It isn't right and it isn't fair. This fact can impede a victim's willingness to disclose and to testify. It can also impede their recovery.
- It really is true that inmates view people who sexually assault children as the lowest of the low. I understand that at least one inmate attempted to sexually assault him, and he was reportedly traumatized by this event.
- No matter what had happened, the kids still loved their father. I think I did the right thing by honoring that and allowing them to have (supervised) contact so he didn't become a sainted martyr to them. Once they were reassured that he was okay and were able to work through what had happened with the therapist, their need to interact with him diminished.
- Honor and embrace the emotions that you experience as part of your recovery - anger, fear, grief, loss, hope - all of it is valid. Don't feel ashamed because you feel how you feel.
- Figure out what will help you to process those emotions in an (eventually) healthy way. You might drink too much, overeat, get into fights at first. Forgive yourself for that and work towards other coping strategies. Ideas: therapy, music, exercise, meditation, prayer, church, talking with friends, massage - whatever works for you, boo. Do that.
-

What I would have done differently

- I would have prohibited Dale from writing to me. I was vulnerable and conflicted, and thankfully my mother stepped in when I could not.

CHAPTER 9
Logistics

*Fact: 23% of all 10- to 17-year-olds experience unwanted
exposure to pornography.*

I kept track of Dale's whereabouts for a couple of reasons. Because of his significant mental health issues, I had (and still do have) a genuine fear about what he might do to me once he was released. His life was in ruins, and he blamed me for that. After nearly 20 years together there was a lot to disentangle. I filed for divorce shortly after his arrest, hiring a local bulldog attorney as my representation. His retainer, in retrospect, was nothing—$1500— but at the time it might as well have been $15,000. I didn't have that kind of money lying around, but I also felt compelled to move quickly. Dale was still disoriented, and I wanted to finalize the divorce before he had a chance to reorient and fight back.

Borrowing money is something I never do, I loathe it. However, in this circumstance I really, really needed to be divorced. Fast. I called my friend Khalid, whom I had known since 1988. I love him like a brother, and he's someone who I knew not only had the resources but the heart to help me. I called and explained the situation and asked for his help, which he gladly gave. I had a check within a few days, which I immediately cashed and wrote another check for the attorney to represent me in the divorce action.

I was still struggling with how to cope with this new reality. I tried so hard to keep things compartmentalized. I made lunches, signed forms from my kids' backpacks, made sure they went to church, participated in the Pinewood Derby with Boy Scouts, got haircuts, and made doctors' appointments. I cleaned my house, went to work, and tried to take care of business. My kids were my priority, but it was hard to keep up with everything. I felt so alone and so overwhelmed with all the responsibility. The irony is that I had already been doing all these alone for many years. It just felt harder now.

I wanted to be strong for them, to just carry on. I am deeply sorry that my children interpreted my coping mechanism of compartmentalizing as a directive to "suck it up." My parents were a tremendous help during this time. My dad took care of home and car repairs, my mom cooked and helped with childcare; I don't know how I would have managed without them.

Diana, too, was instrumental in keeping things going. In the evenings she often watched her brothers and sister as I ran back and forth between home, work, and school. It was a lot to put on an already traumatized child. I am deeply sorry about that too, but in retrospect I'm not sure what else I could have done. I had to finish my master's so I would have the financial resources to take care of everyone moving forward. With the help of my student loans, I was able to keep them in our home and in their schools, but for how much longer could I rely on borrowed money? I worked for many years to pay that debt off and was blessed to have received "loan forgiveness" on the balance in 2022 as part of my public service work.

In 2003 I was working full-time, went to graduate school full-time, and trying to raise five children ages seven to 16. I recognized that I needed help, so I actively tried to identify my needs and supports. Here's what I came up with:

Needs:

- Financial: Student loans—fill the financial void and keep my kids in the house
- Financial: Job—continue to do a good job and maintain employment
- Financial: Extended family—I got a few hundred dollars a month in financial help from Dale's parents, brothers, and sisters in the form of collected donations for the first several months, which was helpful. Once our divorce was finalized and things stabilized, I no longer needed this assistance.
- Mental health: Therapy—to help me and my kids deal with the emotional toll this had taken on all of us
- Childcare: Diana and my parents
- Household tasks: the kids—everybody had to step up

with chore charts. I just couldn't keep up on my own.

Supports:

- Friends—I rotated calls to my friends to vent. Most of them lived far away and could not help with the day-to-day, but they did help me process things. I tried not to overdo calls to any one of them because I had so much negativity and I didn't want to alienate anyone
  - My parents—childcare, meals, repairs
  - Massages—I started going once a month. It was $50 a month and even though it felt extravagant, it helped me to keep functioning
  - Group therapy—one of my classes that semester was group therapy, and I am sad to say that I hijacked the class for my own needs. They were all exceedingly kind and supportive, but it is likely that they didn't get what they needed because I took up so much bandwidth. If you were in that class and are reading this, I apologize for sucking all the energy away.

With these helpers and supports, I was able to keep working, to finish my graduate classes, my practicum, and my internship, and to keep the family going. You may notice that I did not list church as one of the supports. I found that many of the church members didn't know what to say or do, so many said and did nothing. This wasn't helpful, although I am thankful that there appears to have been an absence of open gossip, save the aforementioned woman. My children and I could have used much more physical and emotional support during this time.

My parents were awesome supporters during this difficult time, trusted, stable, and loving adults in our lives. They worked hard to make sure that my kids and my house were taken care of and to fill the gaps that I could not. They were there at every crossroad, taking on many of my responsibilities when I could not fulfill them. I am grateful for their love and service during that time.

In addition to lending me the money I needed for my divorce, Khalid made sure to call periodically to check on me. My friends took turns listening to me cry and giving me a place to be open about my struggles. Jim, one of the youth leaders at church, was always kind and nonjudgmental with my children. He helped one of my sons with his Pinewood Derby project and took another on a Boy Scout camping trip since Dale could not. He always made a point to say hello at church and to be a cheery, friendly presence in our lives. I was grateful for that.

Conversely, other church leaders made sure that Dale got visits in prison regularly but never came to see me or the kids. Neither did the leader of the women's group, nor the head of the regional church group. While I can understand that people may not know what to say to victims, offering succor and support to the perpetrator while ignoring those who have been hurt is unconscionable. To be honest, I am still bitter about the disparity of solace they offered.

With Dale's income gone, there was a huge financial void. I knew that my income and student loans alone would not cover our expenses. As I worked through the numbers and tried to find solutions, I realized that the only answer that made sense was to approach Dale with terms. If he would agree to sign over his 401(k)-retirement account to me, I would agree to pay off all his debts and take the proceeds in lieu of child support for the duration of his incarceration.

He tried to fight but he had no power in this arena. I held all the cards, and he finally capitulated. He tried to negotiate the money, visitation, child support, etc., but the nature of his crime and his upcoming incarceration necessitated his acquiescence to the terms, which I thought were fair. My attorney insisted that I ask for alimony, but I declined. He also recommended child support, which would accrue during Dale's incarceration. I also declined this; the 401(k) money would be enough to get us by. Once he was released, I would petition the court for child support.

The judge asked Dale if he agreed with giving up his retirement savings of $33,000 in lieu of child support while incarcerated and alimony; he did. With an early withdrawal penalty and taxes, the net was significantly less. The divorce proceeding was held in the judge's chambers, with just the four of us as Dale represented himself. We both cried at its conclusion. I learned later that he had sent the judge a letter stating that he refused to acknowledge his authority in granting a divorce and that as far as he was concerned, we were still married. That didn't sound crazy at all to the courthouse personnel who later told me about it.

There were times throughout the two years that followed when I had to go to one of the prisons to get Dale's signature for something—when I sold our rental property, his car, and our family home. I would send them to him via US Mail with a return envelope, postage paid, and he would refuse to sign, necessitating a trip or the threat of court action. I would go because the trips got me what I needed—his signature—but it also got him what he needed—to see me.

Every time I went, the visits got harder. The love I had for him died as the truly disgusting nature of his crimes became more real to me and the shock and crisis normalized into everyday life. As I watched my children struggle, particularly Diana, my anger and contempt for him grew. Conversely, I think his grief and loss deepened, and his social isolation and mental health problems became more profound. He relished my visits, which disgusted me even more. I couldn't understand his lack of shame. His thoughts were all about what he wanted and what he needed; he had nothing to spare for the rest of us that was outside of his interests.

The 401(k) disbursement finally came, and I used it as I said I would. I paid off all of Dale's debts, repaid Khalid the money he had lent me, and paid household bills with the rest of it. At Dale's insistence, we had purchased a Prius not long before Diana's disclosure, so I sold it after he was convicted and bought a less expensive car instead, as well as an above ground pool and a fence around it for the kids. While an extravagance, it was a way to keep the kids amused and engaged while I worked to finish school. I also got a cable subscription for the first time in years. They deserved to have something fun.

What I learned

- Making a list of my needs and resources was an important first step in quieting the chaos and moving out of crisis mode and into a more structured daily life.

- To effectively take care of my children, I needed to take care of myself. For someone else, this could mean therapy, massages, getting to bed at a certain time, talking with friends, etc. If it isn't maladaptive, do what you need to do to get through. I gained almost 20 pounds, finding comfort in food.

- Because our lives were so closely intertwined – personally and financially - I needed legal help disentangling from them. I was only able to get the help I did because I had a friend willing to lend me money. I didn't know at the time that there were free legal services available to people in my situation. I was lucky that Khalid could help.

- While these extraordinary circumstances were playing out, there were still everyday things that must get done. I tried to leverage things like dishes, laundry, cooking, etc. as mindfulness activities – something to focus on instead of the dysfunction. Doing them also re-established a sense of normalcy and structure for my children. I think these everyday tasks and routines helped to close a loop of trauma, fear, and the need to escape because it created a safe and predictable space for them.

- It was important for me to feel connected, heard, and loved. I was glad to have friends to fill that void for me.

- My kids remained my number one priority. I tried hard to not let them get lost in the drama and to address their individual needs.

What I would have done differently

- I wouldn't have kept going up to the prison to get Dale's signature. I should have had my attorney file motions with the court to compel his cooperation instead of playing his games, even if it cost more money and time.

Chapter 10
Unexpected Challenges
Part I

Fact: Emotional and mental health problems are often the first sign of child sexual abuse.

So, Dale was in prison, the divorce was final, our finances were disentangled, everyone went to therapy, and I had help with the kids. Everything was fine from here on out and we lived happily ever after. Sadly, that was not our reality. There were definitely challenges that Diana faced that I didn't see coming and with which I was ill-equipped to cope.

When I worked at the jail, many of the ladies who came to the mental health unit were incarcerated for drug offenses. When they came to see me to talk about their anxiety, their panic, and their depression, most disclosed that they had been molested as children and had turned to drugs and alcohol to escape the shame and the fear that the abuse had created. This escape had in turn made them unable to protect their own children from sexual abuse, perpetuating an intergenerational cycle. Hearing these women's stories made it clear to me that victims need unconditional support and resources to fully recover and progress, but few had the same opportunities and information available to them that our family did. Those women's stories were the primary motivator for me to write this book, to give others the benefit of our experiences and to hopefully help other families recover from this tragedy and break the cycle once and for all, for their children and grandchildren.

I didn't realize it at the time, but many of the disturbing and concerning behaviors that Diana exhibited in the months and years that followed are normal parts of recovery from child sexual abuse. To me, it looked like the bottom was falling out and I was losing my child. Even though I had a theoretical understanding of recovery, I was neither prepared for nor objective about what was happening. She wasn't openly defiant with me, but she was challenging. She didn't want to go to church anymore. She decided she was a vegetarian. Then she was Catholic. Then she was a Wiccan. She didn't like her therapist and refused to continue going. I took her to other therapists but she thought they were all perverts for wanting to know the details of what happened to her. At one point she shared that she disclosed the abuse when she did because Bella was getting to be the age she had been when the abuse started, and she wanted to protect her. Her disclosure had been about keeping her sister safe, not about getting help for herself. I didn't know what to do with that.

Diana is extremely intelligent, and at the time of her disclosure she was attending a hybrid high school/college. She graduated with a college Associates degree the week before she graduated from high school. She had a full scholarship to the state school of her choice. To no one's surprise, she wanted to go to the same college as her high school boyfriend, "Moose," whom she had been dating for several months. I wasn't keen on the living together aspect of going to college together. Our religion prohibited premarital sex, as did Moose's, and they both knew it.

Moose's family was Baptist and well-to-do. His father owned resorts on the coast, and as a young man of means he wanted for little. His parents were not only paying his college tuition but also gave him a monthly stipend in addition to paying for food, housing, utilities, etc. He would not want for anything. At 17 years old, Diana decided that when they graduated, she wanted to marry Moose and go off to school with him in August. They wanted to be together, and they wouldn't get in trouble with their families if they were married.

I wasn't happy about the idea, but neither was I happy at the thought of them living together at school. I remember my mother and I having a conversation with her about only trying vanilla ice cream and that's all. Maybe she likes Rocky Road better but doesn't know it yet. Was she absolutely sure this was what she wanted to do? Today Diana doesn't remember having this conversation, but at the time she was emphatic about her choice.

She had been through so much already that I didn't want to alienate her. I gave her my consent and went with the two of them to the courthouse to sign off. Moose's parents had been married at the same age; they were in full support of the decision. I used the proceeds from the sale of Dale's car to buy her dress, get the food, rent the plates and cutlery, etc. Her grandfather, brothers, and sister helped to build an archway and put up lights. The wedding took place at Moose's father's resort. His parents brought butterflies to release at the end. It was lovely.

Looking at the pictures from that day, they both look ridiculously young—children playing at being grown-ups. She doesn't look happy in those photos. I think she was so driven to marry Moose because it got her out of our house and the memories there, allowed her to have sex without anyone disapproving, and it gave her the freedom she lacked at home. Not surprisingly, the marriage was short-lived. They were not well-suited, and it wasn't anyone's fault. Within two years she had come back home while she figured out what to do next.

On a side note, Moose remarried years later and now lives within an hour of my house, which is remarkable given that we lived in another state when we first met one another. Diana and I had lunch with him recently, more than 15 years on. He and his wife are renovating their home, he is working a job he enjoys, and he has a happy life. I'm very glad that he was able to move forward in a positive way after being such an integral part of our family trauma.

I had moved to another state by the time her divorce was final, and our new home had a mother-in-law suite. I put Diana there so she had some privacy. What I didn't know was that she was inviting people over whom she met on the internet while we were all at work and school. This is another relatively normal part of recovery, but I didn't know that at the time. I was scared for her and for us. She didn't have healthy boundaries, which put us all at risk.

Diana was so very restless. She was desperately unhappy at her core, but she didn't know how to fix it. In the years that followed I have learned a great deal more about Adverse Childhood Experiences, or ACEs, and their lifelong impacts on people's health and well-being. Her traumatized brain was hijacking her ability to heal as it tried to keep her physically safe. Every time she was "triggered" with a memory of the abuse, the fight or flight part of her brain tried to keep her safe by overriding the thinking part of her brain. But we didn't know that at the time. In retrospect, it is something of a miracle that she has not developed a substance abuse problem, something that is quite common among abuse survivors, although she has been known to drink too much when she's stressed. It's so much easier to be high than it is to live with the pain and remember the trauma.

There is an excellent video that explains how the traumatized brain responds to stress. You can find it on YouTube at: https://www.youtube.com/watch?v=ZdIQRxwT1I0.

Diana asked to talk with me one evening, and she told me that she was bisexual and in a relationship with a woman. She had been curious about lesbian relationships, had explored them on the internet, and met Chloe. They decided to move in together and so she was moving out to be with her. I felt blindsided by this disclosure, but I tried to be supportive. Whatever she needed to heal, that's what I wanted for her.

Unfortunately, that relationship was also fraught with drama, including domestic violence, heavy drinking, and living in near poverty. I was relieved when it ended. Diana had not dealt with her demons, and therapy had not helped her. She was spiraling out of control, and I just didn't know how to help. I was truly at a loss.

Diana felt a strong need to be powerful and in control. I believe she thought that would be the answer to the chaos, so she went to the police academy; Investigator Garrett provided her with a reference. After she graduated, she wasn't hired by a department right away and decided to join the Marines. She was a semester short of graduating with her BA, so six times the Marines offered her the opportunity to go in as an officer. She repeatedly refused, choosing to go in as an enlisted serviceman instead. She wanted to prove that she could do it.

As difficult as being a Marine was, in many ways it was the making of her. That branch of the service offered her discipline, a mission, well-defined expectations, and goals—all things that people in chaos need to reset. She thrived within the structure the military provided. While the service lacked the nurture and understanding that she needed, it did give her a foundation and ended her free fall. I was grateful for that. I was concerned, however, about the possibility of her being sexually assaulted by a fellow serviceman, something experienced by 25 percent of military women. Roughly 80 percent experience sexual harassment during their time in the service. Diana reports that while she was harassed, she was never assaulted. She has perfected the "look at me and I'll kill you" face. She's a beautiful woman, but most people who don't know her tend to keep their distance from her rather than risk the ire that her expression implies.

When Diana returned home from a deployment to Afghanistan, she was diagnosed with Post-Traumatic Stress Disorder (PTSD), which she may have suffered from before joining the service because of the child abuse she had experienced. Loud noises, unexpected movements, and crowds all trigger her. When she comes to visit, I know better than to plan a trip to New York City or Philadelphia. Places like that offer too much sensory overload for her to feel safe.

She was home on a visit a few years ago, and we went to a local grocery store. In the middle of our shopping, she suddenly bolted out of the store for the car. I joined her there after I made my purchases and asked what that was about. She said that she sometimes felt overwhelmed and panicked in a crowd of shoppers. She had to get out to feel safe. On the drive home she told me that she feels broken. Her words broke my heart. When I tried to offer her comfort and counsel, she cut me off. She didn't want me to say anything; she just wanted me to listen.

All night long, her words kept replaying in my head—that she felt broken—and with it my own sense of failure as a parent was reinforced. I recalled a conversation we had not long after her disclosure when she expressed anger with me for helping other abused children while not seeing what was happening in my own house. Her anger was surely justified. For so many years I was filled with self-loathing, anger, and disgust over my inability to see what was happening and my failure to protect my daughter. There came a day when I had to choose to forgive myself and let it go for the sake of my other children and my own sanity. All those feelings of inadequacy and failure resurfaced with those three words: "I feel broken."

I wrote her a letter that night, pointing out all her accomplishments: she graduated with a college degree before she graduated high school. She successfully graduated from the police academy and served five years in the Marines in an extremely difficult Military Occupational Specialty (MOS). She fell in love with and married a fellow Marine (he's a very nice guy, by the way), and they are the parents of a beautiful little girl. She won a full scholarship to college. She finished her bachelor's degree. She is half of a functional marriage and an excellent mother to a happy, intelligent, and well-adjusted child. Broken people can't do that. I told her that while she was bruised, she wasn't broken. She shouldn't let Dale take more from her than he already had.

We never talked about the letter, but I know she read it. She left it open on the kitchen counter where I had left it for her. Even today, so many years later, she acknowledges that she has a poor self-esteem and that she constantly pushes herself to excel, even when there is nothing to prove and no one to impress. She believes that she must justify her existence and prove her worthiness every day. My brilliant, driven, and wounded girl. She can't see within herself the greatness that everyone else sees in her. I hate Dale so much more than I can tell you for taking that from her. She was always such a confident, ambitious, and brave child. While she retains her ambition and bravery, her confidence is gone. She is forever changed by his selfishness and the loathsome crimes that he committed against her.

I wish I had understood what was happening at the time. I learned later that all these things and more: substance abuse, depression, promiscuity, anxiety, panic, self-harm, are very normal parts of recovery for child sex abuse victims. Most caregivers don't understand what's happening and sometimes write the person off as "damaged goods." This lack of knowledge can make it easier for people to turn their backs on these children if they interpret their actions to be self-inflicted wounds instead of a desperate plea for escape from the pain. Children who have experienced sexual abuse need to find their footing again while they process the trauma. As caregivers and loved ones, we need to support them through these challenges with unconditional love and regard, consistency, and trauma informed therapy.

What I learned

- The first weeks and months after the disclosure are just the beginning. Recovery can take a lifetime.
- Every victim of child abuse recovers in their own way and in their own time. For Diana, therapy wasn't the answer – feeling powerful was. I learned that she needed to be the one to figure out what she needed to heal, and therapy was not it.
- Out of control behavior and poor choices are often part of the recovery process. All is not lost because someone has made what look like bad decisions to cope.
- Never shame or blame a victim of abuse. It is counterproductive. Instead, I needed to consistently show Diana unconditional love and regard; she already shamed and blamed herself without anyone else's input.

What I would have done differently

- The studies about Adverse Childhood Experiences (ACEs) were unknown to me at this time, so I can't fault myself for not knowing them. However, I should have learned more about what normal recovery looks like and recognized that the things she was experiencing were part of the cycle and helped her to find a foundation. I knew she was in free fall but didn't know how to help outside of getting her the therapy that she refused.
- I should have listened more to Diana when she said she didn't want to go to therapy. I should have at least let her take the lead and either interview clinicians herself or choose not to go. She wasn't ready, and until she is ready all the therapy in the world won't help. Provide resources, but don't force your child to accept them. Best practices now suggest that Trauma Informed Cognitive Behavioral Therapy (TI-CBT) works well to help victims recover.
- For more information about ACEs or to find resources, visit www.acestoohigh.com, www.acesconnection.com, or www.cdc.gov/violenceprevention/childabuseandneglect/acestudy/index.html. You can also visit www.tfctb.org/members to find a trauma informed therapist in your area.

Chapter 11
Unexpected Challenges
Part II

Fact: Children in poor families are 3x and children in rural areas 2x more likely to be victims.

With all the attention focused on the victim in child sexual abuse cases, we don't always recognize that it has an impact on the whole family. That was certainly true in our case. I am incredibly proud of my children for the way they rallied around their sister, for the way they pulled together to help each other through the aftermath while I worked and finished graduate school, and for the way they held their heads up high even though the community knew what had happened in our family. It was tough.

About a year after Dale went to prison, I decided to move out of state. I had a few motivations for doing so. With all the time on his hands, I was worried that he would try to file a motion to get visitation with the kids. He's a brilliant man, and I knew that he would start looking at what options he had, for any loopholes that he missed, or any mistakes the court may have made. He found one, too. He appealed having been held without bond, and the court ruled in his favor.

I was also worried about our safety. Dale was 12 months into his 46-months sentence and would be getting out at some point. If he was released and we were still within the jurisdiction, he could petition for not only visitation but perhaps joint custody. Our divorce order prohibited him from contacting the children because of his conviction, but it did allow for communication if they initiated it, which they had not done at that point. While joint custody was an unlikely outcome, I didn't want to risk it.

Lastly, while most people had not been openly gossipy or hurtful to my children, the fact was that everyone in our community knew what had happened in our family. Everyone knew what Dale had done to his daughter and that he was in prison for it. Everyone knew that he was my husband and my children's father. We were conspicuous in the notoriety, and I believed we needed a fresh start.

I don't think anyone really believed that I would move. My parents thought it was a pipe dream. I had looked at going to a PhD program, but my kids vetoed moving for it. They had friends and family in town and didn't want to leave. I, however, was trying to think about what would happen down the road, and I knew I didn't want to be here when "what happens next" came to fruition. Dale would be released from prison at some point and then be on probation, but his supervision would end at some point. I wanted to be gone when that time came.

I had my sights on New Jersey, my home state. I had been gone for more than 20 years. As a research scientist, Dale went from project to project, so we had lived all over the country. We had been in this community for only five years when the abuse came out, six years in total by this time. My kids had roots there that I did not. To them, it was home. For me, it was another potential battleground. I was looking forward to finding that one place where I could stay for the rest of my life in peace. I made plans to take the kids on a trip during the summer so they could see both New Jersey and New York City and meet those people who had been a part of my life before they were born. I wanted to lay the foundation for a change.

Shortly before we left on this trip, my best friend from middle school, Joanne, had told her brother, Steven, about what had happened and that I was now divorced. He was in an unhappy marriage that was moving toward divorce. To my shock and surprise, I got an email from him just before we left. I had not seen him in 20 years and had only one brief instant message exchange with him 10 years earlier. Knowing that the kids and I were going to be in town, he had asked his wife if she minded him having lunch with us. She didn't, so we made plans for me to meet his two children and for him to meet my five children. I would also be visiting with his sister, his parents, and his grandmother, whom I had not seen since I had left for college so many years before.

Since my divorce, I confess that I was lonely. My self-esteem was devastated by my husband's actions. There were more than a few nights where I drank O'Douls and scanned faith-based dating websites, wondering if I could ever love or trust anyone again. My online dating experiences were actually quite good. I met some genuinely nice people and went on more than a few dates with men I met there, but that's as far as it went.

I remember one weekend trip I took to see someone I met online and my mother telling me to "make sure and take clean underwear, because you never know." I knew. I couldn't bring myself to kiss anyone else, let alone be intimate. I had a few persistent suitors, but there were none whose affections I reciprocated. Two years out from my divorce, it was all still too raw. While I was lonely, I was also mindful of not wanting to bring anyone into our lives who could hurt my children. I wanted to trust people but couldn't. It was conflicting; I wanted to fall in love and to belong with someone while I simultaneously felt too wounded and betrayed to let anyone into my life beyond dinner and a movie. I didn't trust my judgment anymore. I felt ruined.

And now here was Steven, back in the picture after having been unceremoniously dumped by me 20 years before because he wouldn't convert to my faith. We met at the park and he brought his four-year-old son with him. His wife had been derisive about my five children and my pedophile ex-husband – I was no threat to her. We spent a lovely afternoon getting reacquainted. After the park, we got subs for lunch and went to his house to meet his younger child, a two-year-old girl who was profoundly handicapped and was at home with a nurse. It was clear that this little girl was the love of her father's life; he doted on her.

Later the next day, I took the children to lunch, our last taste of Jersey before heading back to Florida. Steven called to see if we had gotten off okay. When I told him where we were, he said that he was only five minutes away and came to join us. He made sure we had directions and snacks and wished us well as we got on the road. His kindness and consideration engendered in me shock and dismay as I found that all the feelings that I had had for him when we dated so long ago were still there. I drove back home with a pit in my stomach, realizing I had made a terrible mistake so many years ago.

After that trip, I went to see my church leader. I told him about the resurgence of these feelings and my worries about being in good standing with God over having them. He was surprisingly kind about it; he had deeply loved his first wife, from whom he was divorced, and understood that we feel how we feel. Nothing had happened, so there was nothing to be sorry about. The question that I needed to answer was this, "Was this loneliness, or was this real?"

Steven clearly still had some feelings for me too. He told my mother sometime later that when I smiled at him, it was as if the clouds parted and the heavens opened. He was miserable in his marriage, and even if there was no hope of a future with me, the feeling of love and joy that he had in that moment made him realize that he could be happy again. His life could be different. He emailed me after I got home, making sure that we got there safely. I told him how I felt. I also told him that so long as he was married, we obviously could not have any kind of relationship. If anything changed, he could look me up if he wanted to. He knew where to find me. And that's how I left it; pining for the same Steven I had rejected 20 years before.

To make a long story short, his marriage ended not long after that visit (to be clear, it had nothing to do with me), and he contacted me again once it did. We courted for about a year via email and phone—he in New Jersey and I in Florida—and in the spring of 2006 we decided to get married. Since I had already planned to leave the state, it was I who would relocate.

I loved my work as a child advocate. I was loath to leave the children with whom I worked and for whom I cared so much. I couldn't imagine doing anything else. I started looking online to see if there was a similar program in New Jersey, and there was. I applied for two open positions in different organizations and was called for interviews for both. I accepted the one closer to what was to become our new home. My mother found a house for sale on the internet, which Steven went to see. It was a 200-plus year old farmhouse that needed lots of attention, but I loved it.

Once Steven's divorce was finalized, we married within months. It seemed rushed to some, but we had known each other long enough and well enough to know that we just wanted to be together. Because of the traumas that we had both been through, I thought it prudent that we go to therapy proactively to help us deal with our individual issues together and to smooth the way for our blended family, which now had two parents, two ex-spouses, seven children, and two cats.

One thing that was unexpected was the communication exercises. Steven and I are from the same hometown, similar socioeconomic backgrounds, and are near-age peers. It took him SIX tries to accurately parrot back what I had said to him. That experience taught me that you can love someone deeply and not always hear or understand them. It wasn't a willful disinclination to engage, it was miscommunication. While frustrating at times, it was definitely helpful for us to go to counseling for a while to work through our issues. It largely got us on the same page with parenting each other's children, communication, and better understanding of each other's perspectives. We even decided to have another child, bringing us to eight, yours, mine, and ours.

My elder son, Marek, had gone to the same hybrid high school/college that Diana had gone to and had a girlfriend, Karen. He adored her and she him. Smart, handsome, and a natural leader, Marek had it all. He was the big fish in the little pond. Leaving all of that to go to New Jersey was not part of his plan. In addition, my parents were vehemently opposed to me leaving. They hadn't taken the thought seriously, and now I had a job, a fiancée, and soon a house. I was leaving, and I was taking their grandchildren with me. It was real.

They urged Marek to stay with them and continue at the hybrid school. They encouraged him to believe that because he was 16 years old he was old enough to make his own decisions in life. As it turned out, he wasn't. I made him come with me to New Jersey and made arrangements for him to periodically fly back and forth to see his girlfriend and his friends. At 16, I didn't think it was in his best interests to be separated from his family. Unfortunately, it wasn't enough for him.

Marek decided to act in a way that would get my attention where his words had not. He swallowed an over-the-counter bottle of Ibuprofen and then came to tell me that he wasn't feeling well. He didn't tell me he had just tried to commit suicide, just that he wasn't feeling well. I rushed him to the emergency room where he eventually told the doctor what he had done. This triggered a visit from the social worker, who told me that Marek could not be released to me but had to go to a psychiatric unit for evaluation. With no other options, I agreed. He went to a children's psychiatric facility for evaluation.

Marek was very different from the other kids at the facility. The staff were quick to point that out to me. While most kids stayed for a month or two for evaluation, he was only there for a week. He was a straight A student who served on Student Council. He was extremely intelligent, well-liked, and socially well-adjusted. He just wasn't the type of kid that this kind of facility usually sees. His motivation had not been to end his life but rather to get me to hear what he was saying—he wanted to go home. He didn't want to be in New Jersey. He missed his girlfriend and his friends. His grandparents would take care of him. He was asking me to let him go.

I heard him, but I didn't agree with him. Once he was released post evaluation, I got him set up with the same therapist that Steven and I had gone to since he was already up to speed on our family's trauma and the dynamics of our household. It turned out that my coping mechanism of compartmentalizing everything had taught Marek to hold everything in and to not show unpleasant emotions. He had to re-learn how to communicate more honestly and clearly. By trying to protect him from my own emotional turmoil, I had inadvertently made things harder for him. I had developed a coping strategy for myself that wasn't working for my son. I needed to find alternative strategies to help, not hinder, his recovery from our family's devastating and difficult experiences.

I was shaken to the core by this event, by my son's scream for help. I called Dale's parents, David and Cordelia, and screamed at them that this was their fault as well as their son's fault. One of their daughters called to chastise me for yelling at them, and I yelled at her too. I yelled at Dale in absentia. I yelled at my parents for undermining me as a parent and putting ideas in Marek's head like "you can live with us," something that I would not and could not agree to. He was only 16, and I had already lost his sister at 17. I was not ready to give up another child. I was filled to the top with fear, rage, and helplessness. It wasn't fair that my children were still dealing with the consequences of their father's actions, and while I had consciously disrupted their lives by moving to New Jersey and getting remarried, I believed it to be for their greater good. Had I been wrong? The scripture about "the sins of the fathers being visited on the heads of their children" took on a whole new dimension for me. This is what the author meant.

With Marek, I tried to be understanding and supportive. I didn't yell at him, I didn't blame him, and I didn't shame him. I could see in retrospect that the trips home had been a bad idea; they had given him a false hope that this was somehow not a permanent move, at least for him. It wasn't his fault that his grandparents had given him an unrealistic option of staying with all he knew, and it wasn't his fault that I had built him a bridge to keep a foot in that world. None of this had been his fault. Like all children in this situation, he had to live with the consequences of the choices that the adults in his life made. Despite his wish to remain with his grandparents, at my insistence he ended up staying with his family in New Jersey. This caused a rift with my parents, who again thought they knew what was best and did not accept my decision about where Marek would live.

The emotional challenges of navigating through our new situation were not unique to Diana and Marek. My younger children Bella, and Jared, started cutting themselves on their arms (Jared now says that he was just following Bella's lead; he's sorry that he tried it). Bella disclosed that she was gay. I wondered if this was a phase, perhaps a reaction to her father's actions, or if it was genetic. I didn't know. (Note: 12 years later, she's still gay). She also refused to go to church anymore, and Jared followed suit. Both showed signs of depression, particularly Jared, who started staying up at night and sleeping all day, even dozing off at school. There was friction in Jared and Steven's relationship from the start. They just rubbed each other the wrong way.

I now had three children in therapy, four if you count Diana's periodic attempts. I chose a different therapist for Bella and Jared, one who specialized in art therapy. According to them, it didn't help; the therapist just played board games with them and asked them how things were going. Jared actively tried to 'freak her out' by drawing pictures of bombs as a way of getting out of going. Apparently either my children were not well suited to therapy or there is a dearth of trauma informed therapists who could meaningfully connect with them. I tried to help by reframing those days with negative associations, like Halloween and Fathers' Day, into days for Disney trips, camping, and concerts, by being open, and by making sure their needs were met. It was something, but it clearly wasn't enough to balance the weight of the damage done.

The only person seemingly unscathed by all of this was my middle son, Angus. He continued to support Diana, but he also loved his father. He was the only one who had any interest in writing to him or getting letters from him, which he did on occasion just to make sure Dale was okay. He still wanted to have communication with his extended family. I allowed it as long as he was interested in doing it and I could review the correspondence first. Emotionally, he seemed to be the most resilient. No suicide attempts, no cutting, no depression, nothing. Just a normal, happy-go-lucky kid who loved band and video games. It was such a blessing for me to have at least one child who was thriving despite all we had been through.

I give Steven every credit in the world for stepping into this mess. There were still adaptations that he had to make to make it work, though. These were not ordinary kids who were the product of an ordinary divorce. These were traumatized kids whose father had molested their sister, was publicly labeled a pedophile, and went to prison. That's a lot of tough stuff to process.

The kids' rooms were upstairs, so Steven never went upstairs if Bella was up there. He wanted to stay far away from any hint of impropriety. He was consciously not very affectionate with them either; he gave them side hugs and never kisses. He didn't want to retraumatize or scare them. Steven is a chemist by trade but a craftsman by birth, and he bonded with Angus and Bella in particular, both of whom liked to spend time learning about how to do things with him. They both wanted a dad, and they were happy to have him serve in that capacity.

Diana asked me once if I was sure that Steven wasn't her real biological father because they share similar outlooks on many things, although they are not close. Sadly, he is not. Marek and Diana both like and admire Steven, but they don't really see him as a father in the way that Bella and Angus do. Jared, who was nine when Steven and I married, desperately needed a dad but didn't click with him like the others had. In some ways I think they consciously work to annoy one another, and while they care about each other, they still have a sometimes tense relationship. I didn't allow Steven to discipline my children, I handled that, and that sent Jared a clear message about the hierarchy in our family. My input was the one that mattered, not Steven's. It's something that still rankles Steven to this day.

That said, there is little that Steven would not do for these children. He fixes their cars, has paid for books and tuition for school, checks out prospective houses for them, has helped them move, makes them spicy jerk chicken from scratch just because (remarkable because he's a vegetarian), and so much more. He shows them every day that he loves them and supports them by serving them in any way that he can. He's just the best of men, and the kids know that he loves them, even if he doesn't express it with "nice talk" (his words, not mine). Steven is derisive of people who talk a good game but don't do good things. His love language is service. My susceptibility to "nice talk" has been cured by my association with him. On those rare occasions when he gives verbal praise, it's because you've truly earned it.

Steven and I had been married for about two years when Dale was released from prison and sent to live in a halfway house for a time. Once released from there, he moved back home to his parents' house. One of his sisters served as an intermediary between us. Through her, I gave him six months to get settled, get a job, etc. before I expected him to start paying child support for the three children still under 18: Angus, Bella, and Jared. Taking all the expenses associated with raising three children, I asked him for $450 a month. Steven and I paid for their housing, insurance, clothing, food, etc. This would cover their extracurricular activities like band, school trips, and clubs.

While Dale was incarcerated, I filed an annual deferment on his behalf from paying his student loans, paid off his debts with his 401(k) proceeds, and kept in contact with his mother every month. He was in a better position than most people transitioning out of prison to start honoring his responsibilities to his children. I really believed that he would welcome the opportunity to contribute to their well-being and show them that he cared about them. Once again I was wrong. The request for child support was the start of a whole new legal battle. Because he couldn't see them, he refused to pay for them. I filed paperwork with the court to have child support ordered. The judge sent us to mediation. I let him pick the mediator. The proceedings were to be by phone as we lived in different states.

At the appointed time, I called in. The mediator explained that Dale didn't want to hear my voice, so he would be transitioning from one room to another, speaking to each of us individually. From my perspective, this wasn't complicated. The mediator and I quickly established a rapport, identified the children's needs, and discussed what was fair. We spent the rest of the time chatting about people we knew in common—he was from New Jersey too.

From Dale's perspective, the length of time the mediator and I spent talking fueled his paranoia. He was certain that I was blackening his name, that I was making unreasonable demands, and that I was working diligently to undermine him at every turn. The mediator explained to him that if a judge were to make the decision, he would pay a lot more than $450 a month as I was entitled to request that he provide support for their living expenses, insurance, money for college, and more. My request was neither predatory nor unreasonable.

The mediator came back to me to let me know Dale's position, which was that since he didn't have the means to pay anything he should not have to, especially since he didn't have any contact with the children. I asked him to tell Dale that I had caved and agreed to $400 a month so he felt like he had gotten a win. The mediator remarked, "He doesn't know how lucky he is. Most women in your position could and would have gotten a lot more." My response to him was, "He has never appreciated how lucky he was about anything. I don't expect anything to change now."

With that, Dale paid his $400 every month. I heard from his family that he often had to borrow money from them to pay it because he refused to work menial jobs, and his criminal record made his PhD and previous work experience useless. He was exceedingly resentful about having to pay "blood money" (his words) to me. While his diligence was undoubtedly based on his fear of returning to prison, he paid in full and on time every month. I even sent him a thank you card after a few years, expressing my appreciation. The money helped a lot, providing the kids with enrichment activities that we would not otherwise have been able to afford.

The agreement was that Dale was to continue paying support through Jared's graduation from high school. In June of that year, I received a partial child support payment, which I thought was odd. I showed it to Steven, who immediately discerned why. Dale had prorated his last child support payment to the day that Jared graduated from high school. It was a stinging reminder of just how petty he remained. I consciously worked hard at never saying anything bad about him to the children because I didn't want them to internalize any of my negative feelings toward him, but it was hard sometimes.

There were other challenges, too. His family had a reunion every few years with his parents, siblings, nieces, and nephews. When we were married, we had regularly participated in them, and they were a source of great fun for my kids. Now that he was out of prison, how could they and he participate? We sent the three kids who wanted to go, Marek, Angus, and Bella, who were by now nearly adults and hadn't seen most of their extended relatives since before Diana's disclosure. They knew about their father and their grandfather's abuse, but they also wanted to see their grandmother, their aunts and uncles, and their cousins. The benefits of going exceeded the risks to them since they were so much older.

Before they went, I set up parameters with Dale's parents that he wasn't allowed around them. They agreed, but once they got there one of his brothers-in-law kept hounding the kids with questions like, "Don't you want to see your dad while you're here?" "What do you want me to tell your dad?" and similar comments. Bella told me that he videotaped them, too. I was furious. It was inconceivable to me that their uncle would be so disrespectful when the parameters of their participation were clear and yet he kept violating that. David, their grandfather, intervened at my insistence and got the uncle to back off. It was appalling and prompted me to sever ties with that uncle and his wife.

This wasn't the only problem with his family. Three of his siblings sided with me and showed solidarity with us, three sided with Dale and felt I had overreacted, and should have "dealt with it in the family." Two tried to be even handed with us both, and one just withdrew completely. No matter which side they chose, they all loved their brother and none were willing to call him out when he was being manipulative, to stop him when he was taking advantage of their parents, or to challenge his version of events or reject his minimization of what he had done. Their family's values of practicing acceptance, forgiveness, and peace inadvertently enabled a culture of abuse.

Two of the siblings who sided with him allowed him to live with their families, and all of them have included him in family gatherings where he has unfettered contact with their grandchildren. Many of their now adult children enjoy spending time with Uncle Dale and, I believe, accept his denials of any wrongdoing, and think that he was unfairly jailed. The ones who sided with me and my children take a more cautious stance, with many of their now adult children refusing to attend events where he will be and who take care to ensure that their children are not in his company, which he reportedly bitterly resents.

I have tried to keep a bridge open so that if the children ever want a relationship with their cousins, aunts, and uncles (who had done nothing wrong), they could. We've had an open invitation to our home to those who want to visit, and three of Dale's siblings and a few cousins have taken us up on that over the years. Steven and I, along with three of the children, visited Cordelia and many of Dale's siblings a few years ago while on vacation. It has been challenging, though. There are divided loyalties.

When the children's grandfather David passed, Marek and Angus phoned him as he was dying to say goodbye, but none of us went to the funeral. I remained in contact with Cordelia, speaking with her every month until she passed in 2019 after a stroke. Over the years, I came to love and forgive her for her choices. When faced with the knowledge that her husband had abused her daughters, she chose him. She mourned him deeply when he passed and did so until her last breath. She took a different path than I, but I understand why she took them. I have chosen not to judge her for that. She was a product of her time, her place, her culture, and her faith. She had her reasons for the choices she made, and they are understandable in that context.

Cordelia asked me to come to see her before she passed and to attend her funeral, which she knew to be imminent. I went and was able to say goodbye. She squeezed my hand, so I know she knew that I was there. Since I made the effort to remain friendly with Dale's siblings, nieces, and nephews over the years, they welcomed me with great kindness and love.

Dale, however, was furious that I was there for the funeral. Even though he knew it had been his mother's request, on the day of her funeral he sent threatening texts to his sisters demanding my compliance with a list of demands under threat of violence against me, which would be their fault (not his) for bringing me there. Already understandably emotional about their mother's passing, they were inconsolably upset. I tried to be understanding of their anguish, but to me this was just another attempt at emotional manipulation. His attempts failed in the end because I wouldn't play his game and refused his demands, suggesting that they let one of the police officers in the family who were at the church that day know about his threats. He backed down. He missed his own mother's funeral because he refused to be where I was, 15 years after our divorce. He'll have to live with that choice for the rest of his life, just as he'll have to live with the rest of his self-inflicted losses.

I recently asked my children a series of questions to get their input on how effective the recovery strategies that we employed had been, looking back retrospectively. Angus felt that the best thing we did was to reestablish a sense of normalcy; for him it was band. He loved it. He and Marek also had a group of friends who came over regularly to play board games. In fact, he and Marek ended up marrying two of those friends. They had a tribe, and they felt accepted in it. He also felt safe with all of us together; he thought it would have been extremely hard for him had Marek stayed with their grandparents while the rest of us relocated. He also felt that I had done a good job of addressing their individual needs. He felt that he personally had attention and engagement from me. The most difficult thing for him was the move to New Jersey. While in the end it was a good choice for him, he struggled with being uprooted from his friends and family.

Marek echoed these thoughts. He too felt that a sense of normalcy and a good group of friends made all the difference. Moving to New Jersey had been a traumatic experience for him, and in hindsight he thought that it would have been equally okay for him to have stayed with his grandparents or to come with the rest of us. He could see pros and cons to both actions.

When asked what advice he would give to other people facing similar challenges, Marek said, "You need to lean on your family. Don't isolate yourself, and don't take on the shame of the crime; it's not yours to keep. You did nothing wrong." Marek felt that the openness with which we handled the situation was "absolutely the right approach," and he never felt personally stigmatized by his father's action. "At the end of the day," he said, "you are in charge of yourself." In terms of his father, he felt that he had the power to choose whether to have a relationship with him, and he consciously chose not to do so. "It's his loss, not mine," he concluded. Marek and his wife have a beautiful daughter that Dale will never see and will never know. It is indeed his loss.

Bella agreed that being together and having a sense of normalcy was important, but she cautions that recovery is a "much longer process than people think it is." While we were open about it in our family, she thinks we needed more therapy. When reminded that she felt that it wasn't effective at the time and that she didn't want to go, she conceded that point but still felt that more help and support was needed to process what happened. She concluded by saying that she knows that she has not healed, but "it's okay to not be okay." She has met with several therapists over the years and has yet to find one who is a good fit for what she needs. In the interim, she is utilizing a web-based therapist and is working to implement strategies like mindfulness and breathing to help deal with her own anxiety. Regarding her father, she too felt that she had the power to choose whether to have a relationship with him.

Devastatingly, Bella has recently begun having flashbacks of abuse at Dale's hands. Neither she nor I knew about this, and we are both back in therapy trying to deal with this revelation. It was another gut punch, but I am grateful that she is at a point in life where she feels safe enough to remember.

Jared also felt that being together, having a sense of normalcy, and sharing family responsibilities were all important. He liked that we had regular family dinners. He was much younger than the others and doesn't remember a lot about his father. When asked whether he felt like he had the choice to have a relationship with him, he said, "Not really. Nobody else was choosing to be in contact with him, so I didn't think I should either." Jared viewed his grandfather and Marek as his "father figures," and acknowledges that he's had a hard time connecting with Steven in that role. He knows that Steven loves and cares for him, which is reciprocated, but they do not effectively communicate with one another overall.

Being part of a large and close family unit had the downside of negating the need for outside friends since Jared's primary friendships were at home. He and Bella are only 17 months apart, and they have always been close and could talk. Jared is charismatic, humorous, and intelligent, and people like to be around him. He easily builds rapport. However, he can take or leave outsiders. And even though they are all adults now, the siblings still play video games together online and group text to spend time together and stay connected. Most of them live nearby and come to our home for Sunday dinner, further cementing their bonds of family and friendship.

Jared is 25 as of this writing, and he believes that our family's experience has impeded his ability to form intimate relationships with romantic partners, and he posits that the overriding barrier for him is fear—fear of rejection, fear of seeming like "a creeper" for expressing an interest in someone, and fear of being hurt. He only recently learned to drive because he didn't want to run the risk of hurting anyone. While he was offered numerous opportunities growing up to do things and go places and was given the tools and counsel that would help him succeed in life, he also feels that I didn't do enough to push him into following through. He got away with a lot as a child, and now, as an adult, he struggles with doing things he doesn't want to do. Not enforcing consequences with Jared has long been a sore point between Steven and me; I freely acknowledge that I didn't enforce rules with him like I did with the others. Guilty as charged.

Jared also pointed out things that he felt we did right: he likes that I have family pictures up all around the house to remind us of where we come from (note: he also points out that I have "too many, which is creepy"), he appreciated that Steven and I gave them the opportunity to make choices for themselves and that they were exposed to lots of different ideas, cultures, and people. He felt that while he was given the tools to succeed, he didn't use them. Jared uses humor and pushes people away as coping mechanisms, but at his core he is a caregiver. He recognizes that he has made a lot of choices to help others that have delayed his own social, emotional, and professional development.

Unlike Bella, Jared doesn't feel like he needed more counseling—"a stupid waste of time,"—but he does recognize that he needs to work out his issues before he can move forward. He is self-aware but often deflects discussions of a personal nature. While our family has been open about what happened, he has never talked to anyone outside the family about it. He wants to date, to marry, and to have a family. Before he can do those things, he needs to overcome his fears, to start engaging with others outside of the family, and to stop being fearful about engaging in normal, appropriate relationship milestones. Jared has been slower to mature than the others, but he is much more insightful and objective about who he is and where he is going than most young people his age.

In short, the crimes against Diana were not crimes against her alone, and the impacts of those crimes continue to resonate, now more than 20 years after they began. There are some who will read this and think there is no hope that things will get better, but they would be wrong. Like Diana, our family has been bruised but it is not broken. There is no doubt that we've had an inordinate number of challenges, but we've surmounted them with time, with unconditional love and acceptance, and with a burgeoning knowledge base of strategies to help us deal with the consequences to both Diana and to our family as a whole.

What I Learned

- I regret my decision to allow Diana to get married so young. It was an escape, not a therapeutic intervention. I let my guilt get the better of my good sense, and I wanted her to be happy. It was a mistake.

- There continue to be far-reaching consequences to everyone in my orbit, from friends to family to acquaintances. I learned that there are some people that I have to let go because they could not or would not support our recovery in the way we needed to recover.

- Diana wasn't the only victim here. The other children suffered too, even though they didn't directly experience the abuse. They all needed individual and customized help getting through this devastating experience.

- It was a challenge to maintain a relationship with Dale's side of the family. For some, blood was thicker than water. For those with whom I have maintained a relationship, it needed to be on my terms where my children's safety and well-being was primary. Professionally, I have had cases where family members have tried to pressure kids to recant to protect the offender or save the family embarrassment. Allowing this abuses them all over again.

- While Dale was out of our family, he wasn't out of our lives. His parental rights hadn't been terminated, and I still had to deal with him on some level. I'm just so grateful I didn't have to deal with a visitation schedule. That would have made the nightmare infinitely worse. I am so glad that the details of my divorce/custody/child support were worked out with the help of a good attorney.

- My kids really needed me to be the leader and to keep them safe – safe from Dale, safe from his family, safe from gossip, safe from want, and safe from themselves. I followed my gut, and today my kids are doing well. I am incredibly thankful for that, especially since my gut instincts haven't always offered the best counsel.

- Counseling was imperative for Steven and me as we started our new relationship. Given all the trauma that we'd experienced, I don't know that our relationship would have survived or been as happy and stable as it turned out to be without it. In retrospect, we needed more guidance on his role as the children's stepfather. He has done an amazing job in an exceedingly difficult situation.

- Even though I managed to climb out of the pit of despair, it is evident that there will always be something that sends me back in. It's a long-haul situation that will irrevocably impact my family forever. It just will.

What I would have done differently

- I wouldn't have pushed Diana so hard about therapy. I should have offered her options and stepped back until she was ready for that step. Maybe other kids are different, but she really needed to be in control of the process, not me.
- I am ashamed that I mourned so much over the loss of what I thought I had. I wish that I had known what was happening. I wish that I hadn't trusted so much. I wish that I hadn't been blinded by love and loyalty. I wish that it hadn't taken me so long to see who Dale really was and not who I thought he was. There are so many things I would have done differently if I had seen more clearly. I am consoled by the knowledge that once I did know what was happening, I stopped the abuse, staunched the bleeding, and provided a haven for my children to heal. The intergenerational cycle of child sexual abuse in that family stopped with Diana, and I am thankful for that.
- A friend of mine told me recently that while I didn't do everything right, I also didn't do anything wrong. I felt that.

Chapter 12
Dale's Perspective

Fact: Perpetrators target children who are trusting and build on that before abusing them.

Research tells us that individuals who sexually abuse children often have difficulty taking responsibility for their actions. Here's a more clinical explanation from Wikipedia:

"A review of qualitative research studies published between 1982 and 2001 concluded that child sexual abusers use cognitive distortions to meet personal needs, justifying abuse by making excuses, redefining their actions as love and mutuality, and exploiting the power imbalance inherent in all adult–child relationships. Other cognitive distortions include the idea of 'children as sexual beings,' uncontrollability of sexual behavior, and 'sexual entitlement-bias.'" These strategies to deflect personal responsibility may make perfect sense to the offender while seeming convoluted and inconsistent to everyone else.

I include the following section for the benefit of those readers who are where I was, struggling to let go of a loved one who has committed an unconscionable crime. I hope that as you read Dale's words, some of the gaslighting and excuses you are hearing at your end are revealed, and the decisions you must make about the relationship become easier.

During his incarceration, Dale had some time on his hands to analyze the situation more critically. He realized that I had cooperated with law enforcement, and he also realized that he might have some grounds to appeal his conviction based on his lack of knowledge of the process. In February of 2006, he submitted a post-conviction relief petition to the court. Here are the remedies which he sought, verbatim:

1. Restoration of defendant's marriage and familial relationships, including the love, honor, trust, and respect that was

present before he was illegally denied pre-trial release and the subsequent disasters that ensued in "domino-effect" manner.

2. If the court is unable to grant restoration of defendant's family, he respectfully requests relief by immediate execution by lethal injection. Without the love, honor, trust, respect, and close relationships of family life with his covenant wife and children, defendant feels strongly that he has no more reason or right to live; for life has become an unbearable burden of shame, remorse, grief, torment, mental anguish, and despair.

3. Voiding of conviction, immediate release from custody, restoration of all civil rights, and removal of "sex offender" designation.

4. Vacate sentence and resentence.

5. As would be expected in fair plea negotiations, reduction of charge...which would result in immediate release from custody.

6. Elimination of all probation, as it is unlawful, vindictive, and unnecessary to prevent reoffense in this case.

7. Correction of harmful error on the scoresheet by removing the unlawfully assessed additional 40 victim injury points (this is double counting of injury, or "double dipping") and immediate release from custody.

8. Rescinding of all "evidence" given to the State of Illinois, ordering the dropping of all charges, and assuring that no prosecution will occur in that jurisdiction; this is to protect defendant from being twice prosecuted for the same crime.

9. Correction of the charging document to reflect the truth of what actually occurred and the narrow time frame in which it occurred; this is to protect defendant against double jeopardy.

10. Scheduling of an evidentiary hearing if deemed appropriate.

11. Appointment of legal counsel for all...matters, including preparation for and representation at any evidentiary or other hearings.

12. As defendant is indigent, waiver of any expenses related to an evidentiary hearing, including, but not limited to, those needed to bring forth witnesses and conduct evaluations.

13. Removal of special condition of probation for Mental Health/Psychological Counseling, as no required evaluation was conducted upon which to base this condition.

14. Removal of special condition of probation of Sexual Offender Counseling, as no need for such counseling was determined by a qualified professional, and defendant had already completed such counseling on his own initiative long before he voluntarily turned himself in for interrogation.

15. Removal of several Standard Conditions of probation...which are unconstitutional, impossible to comply with, vindictive, unnecessary to protect the community, will not contribute to the rehabilitation of the defendant, are violative of probationer's legal rights, and/or contrary to findings of scientific research.

16. Consider ordering medical treatment with Depo-leuprolide acetate or Depo-medroxy-progeterone acetate, rather than probation or sex offender treatment, as recent research clearly shows that such medical treatment is far more effective at reducing reoffense rates, and defendant has repeatedly shown a willingness to submit to such treatment.

17. Conduct the mandatory Pre-Sentence Investigation (although resulting information would now be stale and unreliable to use for fair sentencing).

18. Conduct a comprehensive, retrospective psychological/psychiatric evaluation (though an ex-post facto evaluation may be unreliable in determining former competency).

19. Financial compensation for: loss of wife and children, lost wages, liquidation of assets, loss of investments, destruction of career as a conservation biologist, destruction of career as a college professor, cruel and unusual punishment, violation of right to freedom of religious expression, and immense pain and suffering - all of which would have largely or entirely been avoided had defendant's legal rights not been violated and he had been sentenced properly from the outset, that is, to probation only.

In the end, the court considered ten of these items. What follows are his words; the only changes I have made is to truncate his legal arguments and focus on his perspectives as the text is 53 handwritten pages plus several more attachments that he submitted for the court's review.

Ground 1: The State of Florida, in apparent collusion with the Court, violated defendant's Eight Amendment due process rights by denial of bond and pre-trial release.

On the morning of 07 November 2003, defendant voluntarily presented himself, with no arrest warrant issued, to a police investigator for questioning. Following interrogation, defendant was handcuffed, arrested, and eventually placed, virtually naked, on suicide watch in the County Jail. The next morning at first appearance, the magistrate, via video, informed defendant that he was to be held without bond. Defendant replied, "May I ask why, your honor?" to which the magistrate replied, "Would you like me to read your charges?" Under duress of extreme shame, with other inmates and guards around, defendant meekly replied, "No sir." Defendant was again stripped naked and returned to suicide watch.

The alleged offense occurred nearly two years earlier; the "victim" was initially adamantly opposed to any form of prosecution; the defendant had already voluntarily undergone eight months of counseling for underlying depression and addictions without any relapse; there were no threats or intimidation to the "victim;" there was zero risk to the community; and defendant's family, church, and community ties were very strong, including contractual obligations in two professional positions.

Defendant asserts...that the State and the Court colluded to deny pre-trial release simply because of personal bias against anyone who acquires the label "molester" without any regard for the law, for the rights or the character of the accused, for the best interests of the accused's family, or consideration of the particular circumstances of the presumed crime. This is extreme prejudice, involving taking advantage of the legal naivete of a man who showed integrity by fully cooperating, who demonstrated extreme remorse, and who was an upstanding and highly respected professional member of the community. Defendant also alleges...that he is the victim of egregious discrimination based on the nature of the charges and because he was an educated professional white man (reverse discrimination). In effect, this entire case was handled like a "witch hunt," a calculated and determined cooperative effort between the State and the defense attorney to secure a conviction and long prison sentence.

Ground 2: The State illegally prevented the preparation and consideration of a Preservice Investigation Report, and the court permitted this manifest error, thereby rendering this sentence, which includes "other than probation," unlawful.

Defendant alleges that the State must have had some idea that the defendant had a spotless record and was widely considered to be of high moral character, and this is why they chose to flagrantly violate the defendant's due process rights, having the "prison-at-any-cost' mentality.

Defendant suffered serious harm because...these mitigating factors could not be considered by the sentencing court. For example, 1) Defendant has a B.S., M.S., and Ph.D. and graduated near the top of his class for each of these degrees; 2) worked for over five years as a research scientist (ecologist); 3) taught evening and weekend courses for the Science Department at the County College for nearly four years; 4) held a highly responsible church leadership position; 5) had an excellent marriage and was a "very good father" of five dependent children (all major aspects, both positive and negative, of defendant's fitness as a father should have been considered, not just a single area of intemperance nearly two years prior, for which he showed great remorse, had apologized to the "victim," and had long-since abandoned and overcome through extensive counseling; 6) had a debt load of over $200,000, with debt payments of about $2,800 per month, and a wife who could not come close to making monthly financial obligations; 7) had a history of serious mental illness, including major episodes of severe depression and suicidality, and 8) demonstrated great willingness and motivation to participate in treatment programs for underlying mental illness and to make every effort to overcome addictions which were at the root of inappropriate behavior.

Ground 3: Defense counsel was ineffective by failure to make any effort to secure pre-trial release of defendant and by colluding with the State in violating defendant's right to a reasonable bond.

At their first meeting, defendant pleaded with his attorney to try to do anything legally possible to get him out on bond, explaining briefly his obligations to his family, employers, and students. Rather than filing proper motions and doing everything reasonably possible to secure pre-trial release, as would be expected of a competent and ethical attorney, defense counsel instead offered affirmative misadvice by outright dismissing defendant's request. His excuse for failing to secure this...right was an unrecorded comment..."The State of Florida does not allow child molesters out on bond." Such a biased attitude against the defendant...was subtly demonstrated during each meeting... Defendant's father, who hired defense counsel, stated that counsel expressed "I would not want your son living anywhere near my family." Defense counsel ethically should have recused himself from this case at the onset. Instead, he apparently saw an opportunity to collaborate in ensuring that defendant serve a long prison sentence.

Ground 4: Defense counsel was ineffective by colluding with the State in assuring that no Presentence Investigation was conducted, thereby rendering this sentence unlawful, and by actively preventing the introduction of mitigating factors for the Court to consider prior to sentencing.

When defendant questioned his attorney about conducting a PSI, defense counsel quickly dismissed the topic by saying, in essence, "since you don't have a criminal record, a PSI is not needed." This is affirmative misadvice, likely motivated not by ignorance but by a prejudicial desire to ensure that defendant would serve time in prison.

Defendant held a strong belief that true justice would require a court of law to consider character, background, circumstances, and mitigating factors prior to sending an otherwise upstanding member of society to prison. Applicable mitigating factors include but are not limited to: 1) From the onset, defendant insisted upon entering a plea bargain, motivated primarily by a strong desire to avoid bringing any additional shame or exposure upon the "victim" or his family by having a public trial. He cooperated fully with the police interrogator, completely "spilling his guts" to him and to defense counsel. Defendant refused to sign the plea deal when it was first brought to him, believing that a 15-year split sentence was outrageous. But under extreme pressure, he capitulated two days prior to the sentencing hearing. 2) The capacity of the defendant to appreciate the criminal nature of his conduct was substantially impaired. From the age of 11, defendant was repeatedly exposed to pornography by adults and other neighborhood kids. He became extremely addicted, masturbating sometimes several times per day to magazine images. This addiction became a lifelong struggle, being especially difficult to control with the advent of Internet-based pornography.

Note that research has shown that a sex addiction is often more powerful and more difficult to overcome without intervention than an addiction to alcohol or drugs, including crack cocaine. Also, as a minor, defendant suffered moderate sexual abuse (much worse than did the "victim" in this case) from several others, including family members, and often in conjunction with pornography. Defendant was raised in a family where child sexual abuse was frequent, moderately severe, and continuing over a span of many years. Thus, being "overly affectionate" with the "victim" was not at all perceived as criminal behavior, and incestuous behavior seemed almost normal.

Defendant suffered deep emotional scars from this abuse and developed a dysfunctional perception of what a healthy father-teenage daughter relationship ought to be like. Having been raised in a family devoid of any verbal affirmations or "normal" physical affection, and suffering great emotional damage as a result, defendant was determined to give his own children an abundance of affirmations, acceptance, and physical affection. However, with a sexually mature teenage girl, he was incapable of making a clear distinction between loving and excessive affection.

3) Defendant suffered from long-term dysthymia, occasional bouts of major depression, and other mental disorders for which he sought professional treatment on many occasions. At the time of the incident for which he was prosecuted, defendant was under extreme stress (working over 90 hours per week with mounting debts), suffering from chronic fatigue, struggling with serious marriage troubles (especially sexual) and was very depressed, all factors contributing to poor judgment and a reduced capacity to appreciate the criminal nature of his behavior.

4) Justice to the "victim" would have been much better served with a sentence of probation or other non-prison sanction. This would have permitted the defendant to financially support her and the rest of the family (amounting to paying restitution), assure that the best counseling (including mediation, as deemed appropriate) and minimize disruption to her life. Initially, she was adamantly opposed to any form of prosecution. It was her maternal

grandmother, who suffered through extreme sexual and physical abuse as a child, who did all in her power to pursue prosecution and a prison sentence.

5) The "victim" was a more than willing participant, sometimes initiator and frequent provoker. She often dressed in very scanty, revealing clothing in the home and was very affectionate with the defendant and often solicited back rubs and massages. However, because of her age (13-14), she was likely unaware of the potential negative consequences of these behaviors. Never once did the defendant use force, coercion, threats, intimidations, or promises.

6) The defendant acted under extreme duress and was under the domination of a sexually controlling, insensitive, and manipulative wife. On a frequent basis, she would entice him sexually, then rebuff and reject him as part of her sex power games, leaving him frustrated, resentful, and extremely vulnerable to seeking other sexual outlets. As a very passive, sensitive, and considerate man, defendant did not have the capacity to assert himself and assure that his sexual needs would be met within a very domineering marital relationship. This domination was a major contributor to the perpetuation of the defendant's addiction to pornography, which tragically spilled over, to a limited extent, into his relationship with the "victim."

7) The defendant showed integrity by voluntarily turning himself in to the police, without an arrest warrant, and cooperating fully with the resolution of this offense. In addition, during the interrogation, the defendant volunteered information about the minor incidents, thus he was very instrumental in helping to quickly resolve this case.

8) The offense was committed in an unsophisticated manner, stemming from an innocent backrub. Defendant apologized to the victim several times prior to apprehension and has demonstrated an extreme degree of remorse in counseling, interviews, letters, and conversations with numerous people.

Had defense counsel insisted that full PSI be done and other mitigating factors been seriously considered by the court, it is very likely that the sentence would have only included probation and/or other non-prison sanctions.

Ground 5: Defense counsel was ineffective by failing to order a psychological evaluation, with several concomitant errors: failing to protect defendant's rights to have his mental competency given fair consideration at all stages of the criminal proceedings; failure to file a Motion of Examination to determine competency; failure to prepare defendant for sentencing hearing; failure to ensure that the Court asked defendant the "legal cause" question; affirmative misadvice about the appellate process and failure to preserve competency issues for direct appeal; and failure to have the unlawfully imposed special condition of probation for Mental Health/Psychological Counseling removed.

It is indisputable that several forms of mental illness, including clinical depression, affect one's judgment, perception of reality, understanding of potential consequences of choices, and the ability to completely distinguish right from wrong. Although all accused persons are assumed sane, even if only slight evidence of insanity is present, presumption of sanity disappears and the burden of proof shifts to the state to prove sanity beyond a reasonable doubt.

Defendant has suffered with moderate to severe mental illness since his youth, stemming from a complete lack of maternal affection, "Lost Child Syndrome," other childhood trauma mentioned, head trauma as a baby, and likely other genetic/organic factors. Beginning in 1986, he has sought counseling from numerous psychologists, psychiatrists, physicians, and other counselors in an effort to cope with these problems.

Defendant alleges that at the time of commission of the crime for which he has been charged, prosecuted, and incarcerated, he was not legally responsible for his actions by reason of insanity. Because of serious mental illness, exacerbated by extreme circumstances... defendant was mentally incompetent to appreciate the criminal nature of his acts or to distinguish between proper (right) and improper (wrong) behavior. Mental illness and inadequate treatment (due in part to dire financial circumstances, co-morbid shame, an unsympathetic wife, and strong religious prohibition against taking most forms of medication) severely affected the comprehension and judgment of the defendant and robbed him of the intent that is legally required to be convicted of the crime for which he was charged.

Any perceptive person at the sentencing hearing could have

recognized that the defendant was in no state of mind to be completely understanding and replying to very serious questions. The plea colloquy does not begin to do justice to the tears and trembling of the defendant, nor to the immense despair and fear that severely clouded his judgment. Defendant was there under a coerced plea bargain and went into the hearing with one overriding objective: plead to the mercy of the judge in asking him to consider extreme mitigating circumstances, especially the financial and emotional needs of his family, and consequently modify the sentence to some form of non-prison sanction. Defendant made several attempts to have the judge listen to his plea for mercy, but each time he was thwarted until after all the condemnatory, fateful questions had been answered to the satisfaction of the State and defense counsel. Given his great fear and extremely fragile mental state, defendant asserts that after being cut off for the second time, he fell into a state of emotional shock, cannot recall hearing or answering any questions from that point and was mentally incompetent to understand the rest of the proceedings.

Throughout the legal proceedings, defendant wrote numerous letters to various family members, expressing his deep remorse, shame, depression, and suicidal thoughts. This included a suicide note to his (now ex-) wife, which resulted in a total ban on his having any communication with her or their children and absolute abandonment and alienation by them. *(Author's note: this section went on for several pages, outlining the wrongs done to him by his counsel's failings).*

Ground 6: Defense counsel was ineffective by not preventing the imposition of an unlawfully enhanced sentence which included aggravating injury points-where there were no aggravating circumstances, nor allegation, nor admission, nor a jury finding of such. Further, counsel failed to ensure that legally sufficient intent was established, that influence of a third party was prevented, and that surplusage in the charging document was removed.

The very concept of victim injury is an integral part of the intent of the Florida Legislature in making lewd or lascivious molestation a crime. If there were no injury inherent in this legal prohibition, then how could it be considered a crime? "Victim injury" is a sentence enhancement, a supplemental crime, with a separate punishment attached. Therefore, the "psychological damage" element of this additional "victim injury" component must also be proved beyond a reasonable doubt.

In the present case, defendant alleges that there could not have been victim injury and in no way did his misdeed rise to the level of meriting the additional 40 points (in the scoring done before sentencing) for excessive psychological trauma. Defendant never confessed to any form of threats, violence, scare tactics, or other manipulative behaviors that would merit such a sentence enhancement. On the contrary, he was adamant and consistent in his claim that the victim could not have known of his voyeurism and peeking behavior - to which he did confess. The very day the defendant learned that the victim was aware of his peeking behavior, he quit and never reoffended.

Defendant challenges the assertion that being affectionate, perhaps exceptionally so, with a 13-14 year old girl causes any psychological damage, let alone that level of extreme psychological damage the would merit a sentence enhancement resulting in a prison sentence being increased by 143% for a first time offender. On the contrary, the physical affection, which the victim solicited and to which the defendant voluntarily confessed, could be argued to be both psychologically and physically beneficial. Was the affection shown out of lewd and lascivious intent, and thereby potentially inflicting grave psychological harm, or was it a manifestation of genuine caring and paternal love, thereby sustaining the recipient's healthy self-esteem?

Mere accusation by an angry teenager is legally insufficient to establish the intent necessary for a conviction for this crime. During the interrogation, at every stage of the proceedings against him, and repeatedly to defense counsel, defendant consistently denied that there was lewd or lascivious intent. His motivation was to demonstrate genuine love, acceptance, and affirmation through physical affection, something he was utterly deprived of as a youth. At no time did the defendant attempt to sexually stimulate the victim or ask her to touch or stimulate him in any way. At no time did he suggest that she touch or stimulate herself in any sexual way while in his presence, nor did defendant sexually stimulate himself while in her presence. All physical contact with the victim was motivated out of paternal love, not the lewd or lascivious intent required for a conviction.

Defendant alleges that the poem, which was read into the record by the prosecuting attorney, was greatly influenced "embellished," and therefore tainted by the victim's maternal grandmother. This amounts to tampered evidence and should have been excluded for consideration by the court....In all probability, the victim suffered far more psychological injury by the hysterical response of her grandmother, the apprehension, conviction, and sentencing of the defendant, and the great disruption and turmoil that resulted to her life than from the actual crime itself.

Ground 7: Defense counsel was ineffective by failing to file a motion challenging the allegation of particular facts of commission of a crime by failing to file a statement of particulars, by exposing defendant to double jeopardy in Florida, and to a groundless 3-count prosecution in another jurisdiction, thus potentially rendering both this conviction and this sentence illegal.

The Amended Information document places the date of the crime between 01 October 1998 and 04 November 2003. During this time frame, the victim turned 12 years old. The crimes of lewd and lascivious molestation are statutorily distinct when the victim is, for example, 10 years old as opposed to 15, and the attached punishments for violation of these two laws are very different...It appears that the beginning date of 01 October 1998 was conveniently fixed to coincide with significant changes in the working of relevant statutes—not to reflect the truth.

Counsel's substandard performance left the defendant egregiously exposed to second prospective for the same crime, but under a much harsher statute...all for groundless, non-existent crimes. The defendant did not even learn of these charges against him until 17 June, 2004 when an inmate in the same prison dormitory blurted out to all such things as "child molester...10-years-old...detainer...facing more charges in Illinois." Verbal and nearly physical assaults ensued, and defendant had to be moved.

Ground 8: Ineffective assistance of defense counsel, inasmuch as he coerced defendant into a plea deal by instilling terror of getting a life sentence if he did not sign.

From the onset, defendant insisted upon entering a plea bargain, motivated primarily by a strong desire to avoid bringing any additional shame or exposure upon the victim or his family by having a public trial. He cooperated fully with the police interrogator, completely "spilling his guts" to him and to defense counsel...Apparently, no plea bargaining had been done, as defendant emphatically and repeatedly requested (f counsel).

In summary, especially in light of the defendant's fragile state of mind, he was terrorized into signing a plea deal that he considered extremely vindictive and unfair. Throughout this motion, arguments have been given to show that much critical information was withheld from and misadvice given to the defendant by counsel that could have greatly influenced his decision about signing the plea deal...the plea deal was coerced.

Defendant, especially in light of many mitigating factors, believes strongly that this is a vindictive sentence in at least two major regards: 1) ten years of probation is preposterous, especially in light of the fact that the defendant already voluntarily underwent more than eight months of counseling for the underlying addiction, starting more than a year before arrest; and 2) the victim injury points are vindictive and unlawful in this case.

Ground 9: Defense counsel was ineffective by failing to pursue non-prison sentencing options and by misadvising defendant that no such options were legally available to him.

Defense counsel...stated that no non-prison options were available to him for negotiations. Counsel failed...to discuss all possible sentencing options...[which] include 1) only prison time; 2) only probation/community control; 3) a combination of prison and probation; 4) suspended sentence; 5) community service; 6) out-patient treatment facility; and/or 7) fines.

Counsel also failed to inform defendant of the possibility of pleading to the mercy of the court ("open plea") without signing the plea deal offered by the state...The ten years of probation is especially vindictive. Counsel had an obligation to be informed about defendant's true risk of reoffense (as opposed to widespread ignorance in society at large) based upon: 1) scientific research documenting that offenders in the same category as defendant have one of the lowest reoffense rates among all offenders; 2) the fact that defendant had already willingly and actively participated in eight months of treatment and counseling; 3) professional assessments by court-approved psychologists and/or psychiatrists with reports of specific recidivism risk; 4) interviews of clergy, work supervisors, and others who knew defendant well; and 5) availability of medical treatment options that could further reduce reoffense risk down to less than 3%, and defendant's willingness to submit to these treatments.

Had these and other factors been seriously investigated, together with the needs of the victim's family and society at large, the court would very likely have concurred that defendant was an excellent candidate for a sentence that did not include prison.

Ground 10: Defense counsel was ineffective by not challenging motions to suppress evidence, namely a controlled phone call and defendant's taped confession.

On November 6, 2006, defendant telephoned his wife, using a cell phone, from Tennessee. During the conversation, defendant answered probing questions about his past misbehavior. A police investigator apparently listened in or recorded this phone conversation.

The call originated from Tennessee, and Florida had no jurisdiction to record the call. This was an invasion of privacy. Likewise, there was no court order allowing the interception of this call. Even the "probable cause" reason for the interception of this communication was questionable.

Defendant was informed during interrogation that the police had conducted a search on his home computer, supposedly searching for child pornography. For the same reasons, this was an invasion of privacy and amounted to an illegal search, also conducted absent a court order.

During the interrogation...defendant, on several occasions, said "no," "I don't remember," and otherwise, to the best of his intentions, asked the interrogator to stop, indicating that he did not want to answer any more questions. In light of defendant's fragile emotional state, and especially that he was under the influence of a heavy dose of medication, this amounts to defendant invoking his Fifth Amendment right. Yet the interrogator persisted, until defendant admitted to many self-incriminating behaviors.

Defendant advised counsel of the circumstances surrounding

the controlled phone call and the interrogation and begged counsel to try to get them suppressed as evidence. Counsel outright rejected this appeal with no reasonable justification given.

Defendant was clearly prejudiced by counsel's deficiency in this regard. The interrogator used the phone call as leverage, or a threat, to induce further confessions-in essence, "we've already got you anyway." The interrogation itself was obviously the most damaging evidence. Without it and the phone call, there was only the poem of an angry teenager, who wrote it while she was very upset for being yelled at to clean her room. Had counsel done his professional duty and managed to get the phone call and interrogation suppressed, defendant clearly would have had a very different outcome. It is even likely that a conviction would not have held as there was no corroborating witness or evidence.

Dale concluded this filing with several attachments, including the transcript from his sentencing hearing and letters to and from his attorney. He also submitted with his appeal a document which he entitled, "Timeline/Domino Effect." It was his contention that all of these factors came together to create the situation and should mitigate his culpability.

Timeline/Domino Effect

Note that for the most part, each item is caused by, or at least influenced by (i.e. "poisoned") one or more preceding items.

A. Pre-legal: a few major mitigating factors

1. Very sickly as baby; dropped on head, probable organic brain damage
2. Raised without affection; Lost Child Syndrome, etc.
3. Long history of sexual abuse in the family
4. Early exposure and addiction to pornography and masturbation
5. Dysthymia, other mental illness from youth
6. Emotionally and socially stunted - first date at age 22
7. Domineering, financially irresponsible wife with her controlling, co-dependent mother (MIL) who suffered severe abuse as a child
8. Extreme financial stress and overwhelming debt
9. Overwork, exhaustion, severe depression, deepening mental

illness

10. Coping by escapism - addictive behaviors of computer games and pornography, which eventually degraded to foolish, selfish voyeurism

11. About June 2002 - caught peeking by victim

12. Extreme shame, suicidality, apologies; end of "criminal" behavior

13. Voluntary counseling and treatment for >8 months; no relapse

14. 30-31 October 2003 - victim wrote poem in anger; forcibly exposed by MIL

15. 31 October 2003 - expelled from home; renewed extreme suicidality

 B. Legal: both IAC [Ineffective Assistance of Counsel] and prejudice are clearly demonstrated

16. About 02 November 2003 - wife called the authorities under strong pressure from MIL

17. 02-06 November - Communicated via email with wife and victim; MIL intercepted, interfered; victim's statement coerced, and thus illegal

18. Early November - Business computer illegally searched

19. 06 November - Called wife from cell phone from Tennessee; illegally intercepted by police

20. 07 November - Under heavy dose of sleeping pills, "voluntarily" surrendered to police interrogator without an arrest warrant, without attorney

21. Promised only probation if cooperated, before <u>Miranda</u> rights; delirious, incompetent, invoked Fifth, tape paused- confessional illegal

22. Arrested, put on suicide watch, and deprived of phone calls for 3 days

23. 08 November - First appearance: illegally denied bond

24. 13 November - First meeting with counsel; asked for pre-trial release (denied); protested lies in charging document; IAC from outset

25. 25 November - Request psych eval and PSI (denied): IAC

26. Counsel failed to investigate and file motions to suppress victim's statement, controlled phone call, and confession: IAC

27. Counsel failed to file Bill of Particulars: IAC

28. Counsel allowed filing of false charges in Illinois: IAC
29. Counsel's claim that no mitigation is allowed: IAC (19 Dec.)
30. 15 December - Again demanded consideration of mitigating factors (PSI) and psych eval; again refused: IAC
31. 17 December - Defendant refused to sign plea offer, even under threat of life sentence; insisted on negotiation, face-to-face with State; refused: IAC
32. 23 December - Plea signed by State with no express agreement by defendant
33. 06 January 2004 - Letter of protest, requests, etc. from defendant to counsel
34. Counsel apparently failed to enter plea negotiations
35. 03 February - Defendant signed plea deal under extreme terror of life sentence
36. Affirmative misadvice about waivers, consequences of plea: IAC
37. Counsel illegally prevented PSI, which was mandatory after conviction and prior to sentencing: IAC
38. Counsel failed to prepare defendant for sentencing hearing: IAC
39. 05 February - Sentencing; defendant's intention to plead to mercy of Court obvious from transcripts: IAC for not protecting this right
40. Several violations of Court Rules at sentencing not challenged: IAC
41. Outcome ("poisonous fruit"): Illegal and vindictive sentence of 15 years for first-time offender - violation of equal protection clause
42. Not advised of right to appeal, withdraw plea, etc.: IAC
43. Procedurally time-barred because of affirmative misadvice
44. Functionally unrepresented at sentencing: IAC
45. 27 February 2006 - submitted 3.850 motion, etc.

The disposition of this appeal was that the Court agreed with his assertion that he should have been granted bail; everything else was denied.

In a letter dated April 16, 2004, his attorney sent Dale a letter which read:

Dear Sir,

The purpose of this letter is to advise that at your request I mailed a copy of your January 6th letter to your ex-wife.

Further, I want to advise that my representation of you ended once you accepted the plea bargain with the State of Florida. Therefore, I respectfully request that you not contact me or make other requests of me since I have completed my legal representation. If you desire me to continue to do legal work, I need you to make arrangements to pay for those services.

Sincerely,
(Name Redacted)

I included Dale's perspective for a number of reasons. It's unusual to hear the voice of the accused like this, many of his points paralleled things that I had also addressed, and I think it's important to understand the dynamics of child sexual abuse from multiple perspectives. Shortly after Dale was arrested, we actually discussed writing a book like this together as a way to help other families avoid this kind of tragedy. This is the closest we came to it. I did not change anything in my timeline or in my recollections because of these documents. I leave both accounts in their original states as our perceptions are our realities. I leave it to the reader to decide which one resonates most.

There were a few things from Dale's perspective that stood out to me as differing from my perspective. Dale asserts that Diana was opposed to his prosecution. This was not my experience. She expressed to me a desire for prosecution and for justice from the moment she disclosed to me. Our timelines, too, differ by a few days. My recollection was that Dale left the night of October 31st and returned the morning of November 5th. He remembers returning November 7th.

Dale asserts that the initial report to DCF and his subsequent prosecution were at my mother's insistence and that she was the person who pushed for him to be punished. In reality, my parents didn't know what had happened for several days. It was I who took those actions without anyone's input, urging, or support. I find it interesting that, perhaps because he had been able to manipulate me for so long, Dale seems to presume that I had no ability to think for myself or to take any independent action in Diana's defense. Just as I had underestimated him, he also underestimated me. He mistook my trust for stupidity.

Lastly, it was interesting to find that I was a "dominating, financially irresponsible, and sexually controlling wife." Again, that had not been my perspective of our relationship, nor was it what I thought our marriage was like over the 17-years we were married. I had not read this filing until recently, and reading it now makes me wonder if there was ever anything real in our relationship. I chose to believe that Dale loved me as much as he could with the limitations that he had, but now I just don't know if there was ever anything of value or if it was all a pretense from the beginning. I am ashamed anew over the time I spent in mourning for him.

Chapter 13
Victim Blaming

*Fact: 90% of child sexual abuse victims know their abuser; 10%
are abused by a stranger.*

There was another experience that deeply wounded me, and I
share it because I believe it is a common experience for the parents
of child sexual abuse survivors. A few years ago, I stopped by to
visit a friend who was under the weather. As we chatted, Dale came
up in the conversation. My friend made the off-hand comment, "You
knew what was going on. You had to have. You lived in the house.
You just didn't want to see it, but you knew about it."

I could have taken a punch in the gut better than I took those
words. I burst into tears, my heart shattered. I have known this
person since childhood, and I knew I was loved by them. If they
could think this of me, what hope was there that anyone believed
that I had not known about the abuse? I had failed to protect Diana,
but it wasn't because of a willful blindness. I truly did not know.
And once I did know, I took immediate steps to protect her and her
siblings.

I left as quickly and as gracefully as I could muster. Once I left
the room, I burst into tears again, sobbing all the way to the car. An
exceedingly kind woman stopped me in the parking lot, hugging me
fiercely and telling me that whatever it was couldn't be that bad and
that everything was going to be alright. She stayed there, hugging
someone she didn't know, until I calmed down and stopped crying.
Her kindness, her compassion, and her generosity toward a broken-
hearted stranger touched my heart and soul that day. The world
needs more angels on earth like that one.

My friend can be forgiven for this thoughtless comment
because it was based not in malice but in misinformation. We
humans believe in a "Just World" concept, which means that we
believe that bad things will happen to us only if we do something

wrong and good things will happen to us if we do right. By believing that I knew what was happening, my friend could happily believe that nothing could or would ever happen to their children or grandchildren because their caregivers would know and would prevent it from happening. It is this kind of "magical thinking" that enables predators to have access to their victims.

Victim blaming is something that has come up repeatedly for me, and it undoubtedly has wounded many other non-offending parents and caregivers and impedes families' recovery because it becomes too difficult to be vulnerable and open. My brother accused me of knowing, my friend accused me of knowing, and I'm sure my parents blamed me to some degree for the abuse that Diana suffered because I didn't share my mother's suspicions about my husband. "How could you live in the same house and not know?" Looking back, I can see now that there were red flags that I should have taken more seriously than I did. There is no one who judges me more harshly than I judge myself for having not seen what was happening sooner.

When Diana was about six, we had gone to Florida to visit with my parents, who lived near the beach. We spent the day playing in the sand, running through the waves, and building sandcastles. When we came back to the house, Diana and Dale went upstairs to shower and change. When I came up, I found them in the shower together. I handed Diana a towel and sent her to get dressed, and I ripped into Dale about the inappropriateness of this. He argued that his family of origin had made nudity shameful, and he didn't want his children raised like that; there shouldn't be anything wrong with family members being naked around each other.

I disagreed with this premise. Diana was six and a girl, and I didn't think it was appropriate for him to be naked around her. I made it clear that this was not okay and that he should never do that again. I have since learned that the abuse did not start until she was nine or ten, so this was likely grooming. *Grooming is the foundation that child molesters build before the abuse begins.* They are successful because the average person is often not aware of behavior flags that indicate that something is amiss, and they are often people who are both known and trusted by the child and the caregivers. While not every adult who engages in the listed behaviors is an abuser, these "grooming behaviors" are something which every adult with children should be aware of and look for proactively.

There are six general stages of grooming: Identify a victim, gain his or her trust, fill a need, isolate the child in a "special" relationship, sexualize the relationship, and maintain control. This is what some of those behaviors look like:

1. Taking an unusual interest in a child
2. Making the child feel special and important
3. Cultivating a close and/or helpful relationship with the parent or caregiver
4. Giving a child gifts
5. Finding ways to be alone with a child
6. Having escalating physical contact with a child going from non-sexual to sexual
7. Having off-color or sexual discussion
8. Showing pornography to a child
9. Providing a child with drugs or alcohol
10. Encouraging a child to have secrets
11. An "incremental cultivation" of emotional and physical closeness with a child.

It should not surprise anyone that caregivers often do not see these foundational steps as threatening or inappropriate. They seem like caring, engaged adults who genuinely want to help struggling parents and lonely kids. They stay just ahead of the line so there is a plausible deniability at each step in the process where they remain safe from detection. Once the relationship has been sexualized, the abuser has gained the trust of both the child and the caregivers, making it exceedingly difficult to detect and to prove that sexual abuse has occurred. The abuser often puts the child in the position of having broken rules, like drinking, looking at porn, or smoking. The child is filled with shame because of the abuse but is also fearful of getting into trouble for breaking the rules, making disclosure of the abuse highly unlikely.

I have already described the other two red flags: my mother's concerns about Dale napping in Diana's room and peeping into the bathroom window, which Diana had described as "weird" but hadn't ascribed anything else to it. Aside from periodically viewing adult porn, of which I disapproved, my observations of my husband's conduct were unremarkable for 17 years.

Diana was my first child and she met all her developmental milestones with ease, walking at 8.5 months and talking well before the age of one. She was a smart, engaging, problem solver from the beginning. I recall one camping trip where we were trying to figure out how to hang a bag up high to keep bears away from the food, and she, at seven, devised a solution long before any of the rest of us were able to figure it out. When she was about two and a half, we put a lock on the guinea pig cage because she kept opening it. When I wasn't looking, she pushed a chair to the counter, climbed up onto it to reach the cupboards, took the key out, climbed back down, and opened the guinea pig cage. She's always been remarkable.

When she was about 10, her grades dropped. She became withdrawn, and she seemed depressed. I know now that she was being abused. At the time, she denied there being any problem. I asked for a meeting with her teacher and her guidance counselor, thinking there was bullying going on at school. Nothing there. I made an appointment for a physical with her pediatrician. Nothing there either. In consultation with both, we ended up concluding that it was probably a combination of adolescence and depression, which ran in both of our families. We moved a great deal, and we were going to be moving again, this time from Illinois to Florida. Case closed. In reality it was a reaction to the abuse that she was suffering.

After Diana disclosed, I asked her why she had not said something sooner. I work in child protection, and I taught my children about "good touch, bad touch" starting at age three and told them that if anyone ever made them feel uncomfortable or touched them in their private parts that they needed to tell someone, even if it was a teacher, a relative, or a family friend. I thought I was being proactive. She said that she didn't disclose earlier because she knew what the consequences would be: I would lose my husband, the other kids would lose their father, we would lose his income, and the police would have to get involved. My brilliant, beautiful, wounded child felt that she had to sacrifice herself to protect the rest of us. What a painful burden for anyone to carry, but especially for one so young.

The only other experience that I can point to as being concerning in retrospect was from a class that I took in college. We had been reading about sex offenders, and I remember telling a friend from church about the description of a pedophile that had been in the reading, which sounded a lot like Dale's personality. I laughingly dismissed it at the time, but as it turns out it had been a true picture of who he really is. Even Dale self-identifies many of these characteristics in his appeal filing (Chapter 11).

Here is an edited snippet from Wikipedia of some of the characteristics which many offenders have:

"Child sex offenders often present with low self-esteem, depression, anxiety, and personality problems. Impaired self-concept and interpersonal functioning could contribute to the motivation for pedophilic acts. Offenders had elevated psychopathy and cognitive distortions compared to healthy community controls, and the most marked differences between pedophiles and controls were on the introversion scale, with pedophiles showing elevated shyness, sensitivity, and depression. The study authors note that, 'We cannot tell whether paedophiles gravitate towards children because, being highly introverted, they find the company of children less threatening than that of adults, or whether the social withdrawal implied by their introversion is a result of the isolation engendered by their preference i.e., awareness of the social hostility that it evokes.' In a non-clinical survey, 46% of pedophiles reported that they had seriously considered suicide for reasons related to their sexual interest, 32% planned to carry it out, and 13% had already attempted it."

Dale shared many of these characteristics: introverted, shy, sensitive, low self-esteem punctuated by periods of grandiosity, often depressed, preferred the company of children, and made excuses for his poor behavior. I believe I was truly his only real friend. He had great difficulty making and maintaining relationships with his peers, only connecting with others if they shared an interest of his. He preferred to be home with me and the children above all else. It was not until I gained both life experiences and a formal education that I learned about codependent relationships, grooming behaviors, and the psychological profile of a child molester. How could I not have known? Because Dale did not want me to know, and I didn't know enough to suspect that anything was amiss.

Please, be gentle with those who have been manipulated, lied to, humiliated, and betrayed. Whether it is by a cheating spouse, a thieving partner, or an abusive loved one, the people who have been manipulated have been abused by individuals who are master manipulators, people who are experts at gaslighting and fooling the people who love them. We're already devastated, ashamed, embarrassed, and humiliated. We don't need anyone else's judgment as we're busy dealing with our own. Thanks.

Chapter 14
Today

Fact: Recovery is possible, and victims and their families can be happy again.

Today my life is good. I am still happily married to Steven, who has accepted our family's trauma and baggage for the love of me. Our eight children are all doing well and are happy. We have three grandchildren as of this writing. We still live in our old and rambling farmhouse. I am engaged in work I find meaningful and that I am passionate about, and I feel like I am making a difference in the lives of abused and neglected children in my community by teaching others about the impacts of trauma on children, child sexual abuse prevention, and how to support the needs of abused children. I am well educated with a graduate degree, have won awards and accolades for my work, and have the credentials of a respected professional. I have friends and family who love me and support me. I could not ask for more than I have.

Getting here has not been easy, and I could not have predicted in 2003 that my life could or would ever be this good again. I wrote this memoir/recovery guide to give other families like mine hope that things will get better. Today my children are healthy, happy, stable, and responsible adults. The married ones have good relationships with their spouses and are excellent parents to their children. They work. They pay their bills. Pre-Covid, they came for Sunday dinner to visit with Steven and me and with each other. The intergenerational cycle of child sexual abuse has been stopped. It is my prayer that my grandchildren's life experiences will be hugely different from their parents.'

As hopeless and mind-numbingly bleak as things seemed when I learned the truth about what had happened in my family on that long-ago Halloween, we have largely recovered from this trauma. Most importantly, they are better for my precious child. Diana still struggles, but she is successful in everything she tries. She is happily working in engineering as a respected professional, she is half of a happy marriage, and she is an excellent parent to her daughter. She is winning the battle, even on those days when she doesn't feel like she is making progress.

I am saddened, though, by the challenges that she still faces, challenges that she neither asked for nor deserves, the panic, the anxiety, and the feeling that she still must prove herself worthy. Every day she is the first one up, she is the one who works the hardest and the longest, and she is the last one done. She never seems to be okay with just being, and I worry about that. And now I am worried about Bella, too.

Reading Dale's bitter argument that he was unfairly assessed 40 victim injury points in his sentencing because what he did to her didn't really hurt her sickens me. He even went so far as to have his mother send me a handwritten scoresheet, ranging from acts of "violent rape with injury" to "appropriate hugs," and asked me to have Diana rank his acts against her in the hopes of getting a reduction in victim injury points to lessen his sentence. I sent it to the prosecutor instead.

Diana can't see how remarkable she is, not for what she does but just for who she is. She is so remarkable that one year I got a Mother's Day card from HER mother-in-law thanking me for raising such an amazing daughter who's a hard worker, a thoughtful person, and a good wife to her son and a loving and patient mom to her granddaughter. Getting that card was one of the proudest moments of my life. Learning about Dale's role in wounding her so deeply is my most devastating wound.

I am a person of deep faith, and in my darkest hours I pleaded with God for an explanation as to why we went through this. I had been so certain that I was doing everything that was expected of me, and yet these terrible things happened to my daughter and to my family. The impression that I got was that this was a sickness in that family that needed to be stopped, and that Diana and I were going to stop it. Even though I eventually left my church, I have not ceased to believe that God was with me throughout this experience and had a hand in nudging me back to school so I could financially take care of my children, in assigning Investigator Garrett to our case—he was the right man at the right time—and for bringing Steven back into my life just when I needed him most. Despite our suffering, I have been blessed many times over. God knew my name.

Forgiveness is an aspect of my experience that I did not meaningfully address, perhaps because I don't know if I'm fully there yet. I feel that I've largely forgiven Dale for what he's done to us, not for his sake but for mine. He rarely crosses my mind anymore, and the vitriol that welled up unbidden in the early days has died. Living with so much anger, betrayal, and hate had its place in allowing me to detach emotionally, but it would have warped me into someone I didn't want to be had I allowed those feelings to remain and grow. I cannot speak for Diana and whether she's reached a place of forgiveness, but I needed to in order to be there for my children. The burden we carry when we don't forgive gives the offender a permanent place in our hearts and in our minds. I didn't want to give Dale that much power over my life. There's a reason that God tells us to forgive - it heals us.

When I wrote my master's thesis, my original intention was to write a guide for families who had been through the experience of child sexual abuse in their families. While we have pockets of resources in our communities, there are inequities in services and so much shame attached to the crime that too many people don't get the help they need. I ended up switching the focus to a comparison of services for victims between northwest New Jersey and northwest Florida. One intervention that I did not address in our family's story is psychosexual education to help children learn about healthy sexuality, personal boundaries, respecting others' boundaries, and how to protect themselves from future abuse. There are significantly higher rates of child sexual abuse among children whose mothers had been sexually abused as children and repeat victimization for those who have previously been abused. Information is power, and sharing the dynamics that enable abuse to occur will help to end that intergenerational cycle.

I would also refer you to The Body Keeps the Score by Bessel van der Kolk about the impacts of childhood trauma on children's development. It has a lifelong impact, but those impacts can be mitigated once you understand what's happening to you physiologically.

Because there is so much shame attached to this crime, there is a dearth of resources for non-offending parents and even fewer people who are willing to share their stories. I wrote this memoir with as much transparency and openness as I could to show my support and share my hard-earned experience with other families who have gone through the same nightmare that we have been through. As someone who is trained as a clinician, who works in child welfare, and who has been on the other side of the table as a non-offending parent, I believe that I am in a unique position to offer some insights and practical tips on recovery. I hope the information I have shared will help put your experience into context and offer support and resources as you recover.

Living through this nightmare has changed me. One of the greatest gifts that I have received is the lesson to not judge others. My previously held "Just World" notions of good and bad behaviors have changed. I no longer condemn people who abuse drugs and alcohol, are promiscuous, overeat, or who have emotional or behavioral challenges. I now try to look at people through a trauma informed lens and see these actions for what they often are: unhealthy coping mechanisms for people who have been deeply wounded and are trying to heal but are struggling to find a healthy way to do it. In the words of Maya Angelou, "Do the best you can until you know better. Then when you know better, do better." A colleague recently told me that he viewed me as an activist. I've never thought of myself that way, but I'm embracing it.

Please don't feel alone. Others have walked these same floors and have come out the other side. If you are doing well and want to help others, please consider volunteering with your local CASA or Guardian ad Litem program, Big Brothers/Big Sisters, or child advocacy center. There are too many children out there without a voice, and the biggest predictor of a child's recovery from experiences like these is a positive relationship with a caring, stable, and engaged adult. Take the steps you need to help and heal yourself, your children, and your family so you can be that person for a child who needs you. God bless you and your family.

Tracey

Appendix A
Helpful Tips

- Believe your child. The statistics overwhelmingly support their truthfulness.
- Reassure your child of your love and support. They are not to blame for what happened.
- Ensure the child's physical and emotional safety from the offender and the offender's allies.
- Notify either law enforcement or child protective services once you learn of the allegations.
- Cooperate fully with the subsequent investigations.
- Identify your support network. You'll need them.
- Utilize the services that are immediately available to you – child advocacy center, local sexual assault center, etc. – they can help with the immediate therapeutic needs and set your family up for longer-term services.
- If the therapist isn't a good fit, keep looking until you find someone who is. The person you select should have expertise in trauma recovery and Post-Traumatic Stress Disorder.
  *If your child isn't ready for counseling, don't force them to go.
- Don't forget that this is a crime that impacts the whole family – make sure everyone is getting support services. Again, offer resources but don't force them to go.
- Make sure that you are getting counseling too – feeling like an inadequate failure is not uncommon. Your kids need you – do what you need to do to take care of yourself.
- If the offender was someone who contributed to the household needs, investigate local resources that can help in lieu of that person's economic contributions. HUD Housing assistance, SNAP (Supplemental Nutrition Assistance Program [food stamps]), local food banks, WIC (Women's Infants and Children), are all good national resources.
- Recognize that if the offender was someone in your family,

you may grieve and feel a profound sense of loss. It eases with time and distance.

• Your child may exhibit some negative and frightening behaviors or reactions because of the abuse. Things like drug use, promiscuity, self-harm, anger, withdrawal – they are all normal responses to child sexual abuse.

• If you see some of these behaviors, understand that your child is not a bad person trying to upset you. They are a wounded child struggling to figure out how to deal with a traumatic and terrible event. Now, more than ever, they need your love, your support, and your understanding. Don't punish or shame them. Be patient. Find them psychosexual education classes, trauma informed therapy, and learn how to interact with them in a way that builds their resilience and self-esteem.

• Your family should have a frank discussion about how you want to handle what has happened in your family. I caution against family secrets – they inadvertently foster a sense of shame and damage, particularly for victims.

• Unconditional love, support, and acceptance should be the overriding messages you give your child.

• With 1/13 boys and 1/4 girls (per the CDC) having been victims of child sexual abuse by age 18, there are other parents in your community who are dealing with this too. Look for a support group where you can freely share your struggles with recovery.

You are braver than you believe, stronger than you seem, and smarter than you think.
Christopher Robin, *Winnie the Pooh*

Appendix B
Additional Resources

Information about child sexual assault and recovery
- National Sexual Assault Hotline, 800.656.HOPE (4673)
- Darkness to Light Child Abuse Statistics (source of the Facts at the beginning of each chapter), http://www.d2l.org/wp-content/uploads/2017/01/all_statistics_20150619.pdf
- RAINN, Rape, Abuse, Incest National Network, www.rainn.org
- National Center for Victims of Crime, http://victimsofcrime.org/help-for-crime-victims/get-help-bulletins-for-crime-victims/bulletins-for-teens/child-sexual-abuse
- The Mama Bear Effect, http://www.themamabeareffect.org/support-the-victim.html
- *The Body Keeps the Score* by Bessel van der Kolk
- List of Trauma Informed practitioners, by state, https://tfcbt.org/members/

Information about economic support resources
- Women Infants and Children (WIC), https://www.fns.usda.gov/wic/women-infants-and-children-wic
- Housing and Urban Development (HUD), https://www.hud.gov/
- Supplemental Nutrition Assistance Program (SNAP), https://www.fns.usda.gov/snap/supplemental-nutrition-assistance-program-snap
- * Aunt Bertha, guide to free or reduced goods/services, https://www.auntbertha.com/
- * Legal Aid, https://www.usa.gov/legal-aid

Support for Parents
- Mothers of Sexually Abused Children,
   http://www.mosac.net/
- *When Your Child Has Been Molested: A Parent's Guide to Healing and Recovery* by Kathryn Hagans and Joyce Case
- Stop It Now!
   https://www.stopitnow.org/ohc-content/resources-for-parents-of-survivors
- Circle of Moms,
   https://www.circleofmoms.com/mothers-of-sexually-abused-children

About the Author

Tracey Wilson Heisler, MA, has worked with families in crisis since 1988. She holds a BA in Psychology with minors in Forensics and Juvenile Justice and a MA in Counseling Psychology from the University of West Florida. Her professional experience includes working with victims of domestic violence, sexual assault, and child abuse and neglect as well as supporting the recovery efforts of juvenile and adult offenders. Her breadth of experience informed her family's recovery from child sexual abuse. She is a long-time child advocate who has made a lifetime commitment to disrupting ACEs and promoting resilience and recovery.

Printed in the USA
CPSIA information can be obtained
at www.ICGtesting.com
BVHW051415080823
668344BV00005B/13